SHERRY LYNN MIMS JIMÉNEZ is a certified childbirth educator who specializes in perinatal grief counseling and is a contributing editor for *American Baby Magazine*. She teaches holistic childbirth education, which she refers to as the New Lamaze. In addition, she has lectured to health professionals and parents and written numerous articles and books, including *Childbearing: A Guide for Pregnant Parents*, published by Prentice-Hall, Inc.

THE OTHER SIDE OF
PREGNANCY
Coping With Miscarriage and Stillbirth

Sherry Lynn Mims Jiménez

A SPECTRUM BOOK

PRENTICE-HALL, INC. Englewood Cliffs, N. J. 07632

Library of Congress Cataloging in Publication Data

Jiménez, Sherry Lynn Mims.
    The other side of pregnancy.

    "A Spectrum Book."
    Bibliography: p.
    Includes index.
    1. Miscarriage—Psychological aspects. 2. Still-
birth—Psychological aspects. 3. Perinatal mortality—
Psychological aspects. 4. Bereavement. I. Title.
RG648.J6   155.9'37   82-426
ISBN 0-13-643163-1   AACR2
ISBN 0-13-643155-0 (pbk.)

For Angel, Daniel, and Amy Rebecca, as always,
and for every mother and father who have wept for a lost baby.

A SPECTRUM BOOK

Excerpts on p. 31 and 68 from *Swimmer in the Secret Sea* by William Kotzwinkle
reprinted by permission of the author. Copyright © 1975 by William Kotzwinkle.
Excerpt on pp. 131-132 reprinted from *Birth* by Caterine Milinaire
with permission of Harmony Books. Copyright © 1974 by Caterine Milinaire.

ISBN 0-13-643155-0 {PBK}

ISBN 0-13-643163-1

10 9 8 7 6 5 4 3 2 1
Printed in the United States of America
Editorial/production supervision by Cyndy Lyle Rymer
Manufacturing buyer Barbara Frick
Cover design by Jeannette Jacobs

Prentice-Hall International, Inc., *London*
Prentice-Hall of Australia Pty. Limited, *Sydney*
Prentice-Hall of Canada Inc. *Toronto*
Prentice-Hall of India Private Limited, *New Delhi*
Prentice-Hall of Japan, Inc., *Tokyo*
Prentice-Hall of Southeast Asia Pte. Ltd., *Singapore*
Whitehall Books Limited, *Wellington, New Zealand*

CONTENTS

PREFACE

This is a practical guide for people who must cope with the tragedy of miscarriage or stillbirth. It offers help and hope to the parent who has lost a baby. Families, friends, and health professionals will find here the information and reassurance they need to comfort the parents and promote the healing process.

Here you will discover effective ways to deal with the overwhelming emotions that can engulf the parent whose baby dies. By understanding why you sometimes feel like crying or screaming or just doing nothing, you will be able to acknowledge and accept these feelings as normal. This is the first step toward learning to deal with grief. Knowing that other parents experience feelings of guilt, anger, and depression can help you relax and move on towards mending your life.

This book will answer your many questions about what happened. By looking into the various causes of miscarriage and stillbirth, you can reassure yourself about the future. Most parents find that when they understand the facts, they are less afraid and can stop feeling guilty and fearful that they did something to hurt the baby.

As you read this book, you will be guided step by step through the phases of recovery from both miscarriage and stillbirth. You will see how other parents describe what happened when their own babies died, and you will follow them through the aftermath as they explain the impact of this loss on their own personal lives and on their marriages and families. They will tell you how their friends and the health professionals around them reacted, and how these responses helped or hurt. Woven throughout these parents' comments are explanations to help you use their experiences for your own benefit.

One of the most useful aspects of this book is its practical approach. Not just a book of theories and concepts, it is filled with constructive suggestions to help you ease back into the flow of your daily life.

A special chapter is written just for health professionals. Nurses, doctors, ministers, and counselors will find the information and ideas they need to help parents and families deal with the events of miscarriage and stillbirth. Gathered from parents as well as professionals, these suggestions will demonstrate how others have offered productive support and comfort from the prenatal period through labor, delivery, and postpartum. Throughout the book, health professionals will discover ways to assist in the long-term recovery.

Other special features include a glossary of medical terms and a bibliography of books and articles of interest to both parents and professionals. There is also a chapter dealing with the next pregnancy. Here you will find information on tests and precautions your doctor might take to help insure the safety of you and your baby. You will follow several couples who told their stories in earlier chapters as they go on to have healthy children.

The myths and fears surrounding birth and death have created a conspiracy of silence. This has made it difficult for people to talk about these subjects, and almost impossible to find the answers you are seeking. In reading *The Other Side of Pregnancy*, you will realize that birth and death are integral parts of each family's life cycle. As you begin to understand more about miscarriage and stillbirth, you will be able to accept and deal with the grief that occurs when there is not time between the birthing and the dying. You will discover that a grieving parent has an intense need to have others recognize that this baby was important and that his loss will be felt and remembered.

The days, weeks, and months ahead will not be easy, but you can make it. There will be a lessening of grief as time goes by. You will never forget your baby, but one day you will find that you can think and talk about him with a sense of peace and acceptance. Reading this book is an important step.

ACKNOWLEDGMENTS

This book is the brainchild of no one person—it is the heartchild of many. I owe a special debt of gratitude to the mothers and fathers with whom I have worked and whose stories appear on these pages. Two of these women deserve an added thank you: Susan Blackwell, whose experience was the catalyst for the creation of this book, and Aggie Stryker, whose valuable insights have inspired me throughout my career.

While writing this book I struggled with certain chapters until I almost gave up. Each time I was ready to quit, there would come a phone call from Heather Gladden. A newly graduated nurse, her constant questioning of the medical and nursing care of high-risk maternity patients at her hospital kept me on my toes and usually gave me just the material I needed to overcome my writer's block.

Stillborn

I carried you in hope,
the long nine months of my term,
remembered that close hour when we made you,
often felt you kick and move
as slowly you grew within me,
wondered what you would look like
when your wet head emerged,
girl or boy, and at what glad moment
I should hear your birth cry,
and I welcoming you
with all you needed of warmth and food;
we had a home waiting for you.

After my strong labourings,
sweat cold on my limbs,
my small cries merging with the summer air,
you came. You did not cry.
You did not breathe.
We had not expected this;
It seems your birth had no meaning,
or had you rejected us?
They will say that you did not live,
register you as stillborn

But you lived for me all that time
in the dark chamber of my womb;
and when I think of you now,
perfect in your little death,
I know that for me you are born still;
I shall carry you with me forever,
my child, you were always mine,
you are mine now.

Death and life are the same mysteries.

Leonard Clark

INTRODUCTION

"Linda had the baby this morning. It was stillborn."

Tom waited silently for my response. I wanted to tell him everything would be all right—that he and Linda would survive this experience and rebuild their hopes for a family. But, for the moment, all I could say was, "I'm sorry."

This was the phone call I had expected and feared ever since I began teaching pregnant parents in childbirth education classes. Until now, I had beaten the odds. Couples come to me with the expectation that I will help them prepare for a memorable and joyous birth. Usually that is exactly what happens.

Even when things do not go as well as anticipated, such as in a Cesarean or a premature birth, the parents feel prepared to cope. But no amount of planning and teaching can prepare them for the disillusionment and emptiness that accompany the loss of the baby. We all know that some babies do not make it, but no mother or father expects his or her own to be the one. It just cannot happen.

When it does happen, the parents feel angry and hurt and guilty and frustrated, and they must deal with these feelings alone. Families and friends do not know how to help. They want the grief-stricken couple to be happy again. They tell them to "put this behind you and start over." They say, "The sooner you forget about it, the better." And, worst of all, "You can always have another baby."

No one seems to understand that the grieving man and woman will never forget, that they do not want another baby—they want *this* one.

Even health professionals are not always equipped to handle their own feelings of failure. They avoid the anguished family. Ostracizing the mother from the postpartum ward, they place her on a distant floor where the staff may not know how to care for a woman who has just lost her baby. Instead of receiving professional support and counseling, she is shuffled out of the hospital as soon as possible. The distressed woman asks, "What now?" Her doctor answers, "I'll see you in six weeks."

There can be an even greater lack of understanding and support for parents who have experienced a miscarriage. My first formal education regarding fetal death came from a high school home economics teacher who taught a short unit on reproduction. (For most of us this would be the extent of our sanctioned sex education.) She was more concerned that we learn the etiquette of baby showers than the more intimate details of reproduction. She cautioned us about the timing of announcing a pregnancy: "Wait until the third month is over before telling anyone, even your own parents. This way, if you should miscarry, you won't have to worry about whether to return the gifts. If you had already had a baby shower, it would be embarrassing for everyone."

She compared losing a baby with breaking an engagement and having to give back all the presents. After all, some would say, it is not as if they lost a baby. Or is it? Isn't miscarriage just another form of stillbirth?

Why is it so difficult to handle our feelings about someone

else's tragedy? What, or who, created this conspiracy of silence surrounding miscarriage and stillbirth?

We are frightened of death. It reminds us of our own mortality. When a child dies, we must face the vulnerability of our own children. Perhaps one of the greatest fears of any parent is that his child will precede him in death. Studies show that the loss of a child has a greater impact on a person than the death of a spouse.

The loss of a young person affects society as well as the individual. A child's death symbolizes lost potential—what might have been. The death of an infant who had no real chance to live is perhaps the greatest insult of all.

Left alone, the grieving family must make some sense out of what happened in order to rebuild their lives and go on. This book is written to offer hope and help to these people, and guidance to those who know and love them. The information herein has been repressed in the past by the benevolent conspiracy of silence. The members of the conspiracy have, until now, been anonymous, unaware even of their own involvement. They have included the doctor, the nurse, the childbirth educator, the friends and family of the bereaved, and sometimes even the bereaved pair themselves. Together, we form society. If society's attitude toward miscarriage and stillbirth is to change, it must begin with the individual. The individuals described in this book have made a significant beginning by sharing their mutual loss, as well as the steps they took toward recovery.

AN ORIENTATION

CHAPTER
1

The young, black woman moaned rhythmically with each wave of pain and nausea. She was five months pregnant, and her baby was on his way now. I, the inexperienced student nurse, was assigned to care for her. The head nurse said, "Don't pay attention to her noise. She's just trying to get sympathy."

Later I asked if the woman could have something to ease her pain. The head nurse said, "There's nothing wrong with her. Just leave her alone. She thinks she is in labor, but she doesn't know what's going on."

When the lunch trays arrived, there was one with her name on it. I asked why. We usually did not give full meals to women in labor. The head nurse said, "She is not in labor. I haven't felt any genuine contractions all morning. Just take her the tray and tell her to eat."

I carried the lunch tray into the tiny, drab cubicle where the woman lay, still moaning, now writhing, in pain. "Are you all right?" I asked.

She looked at me with big, frightened eyes and said, "I think I had the baby."

I pulled back the sweaty sheets and saw a perfectly formed, miniature black baby, lying still and quiet and dead.

One-fifth of all pregnancies end in spontaneous abortion, or miscarriage. There are about 500,000 miscarriages yearly in the United States. Of these, one-third occur before the mother is aware she is pregnant. This means that each year well over 300,000 couples lose babies that had already become a physical and emotional reality for them—babies for whom they had begun planning the welcome home. Another 200,000 lose their babies before they ever realized their existence.

Approximately one or two out of every 100 babies are stillborn. Although data vary due to disagreement over the exact definition of stillbirth, probably 60,000 or more babies are born dead each year in the United States.

There are several myths and many misunderstandings about miscarriage and stillbirth. These add to our difficulty in coping with the aftermath. Clear definitions of the language of both normal and abnormal pregnancy will help eliminate these misapprehensions.

THE TERMINOLOGY OF PREGNANCY

During the first two months of pregnancy, the developing child is called an *embryo*. Afterwards, the child is referred to as the *fetus*. In the past, the word *abortion* was commonly used to describe the birth of a nonviable fetus, or one who cannot support life on her own systems. Medical books now refer to any embryo or fetus that is born before the twentieth week, or weighing less than 500 grams (one pound one ounce), as having been aborted. Because the word miscarriage is widely used among lay people, probably due to the stigma sometimes attached to the word abortion, we will use the two terms interchangeably.

An *induced abortion* is one that is intentionally accomplished by mechanical or medical means. A *spontaneous abortion* is one that occurs without human intervention.

Threatened abortion is a situation in which a woman has early signs of miscarriage, such as cramping and vaginal bleeding before the twentieth week of gestation. Sometimes the pregnancy can be maintained with the use of bedrest and drugs, but often it is impossible to prevent the miscarriage. *Inevitable abortion* means that, besides cramping and bleeding, the woman's cervix has undergone some of the changes necessary to expel the fetus.

In an *incomplete abortion* some portion of the fetus, membranes, or placenta has been retained within the uterus. This will have to be removed by a physician. The usual procedure is to do a dilatation and curettage (D and C). This involves the dilatation of the cervix in order to scrape, or curette, the uterine cavity. A D and C is usually done in a hospital while the patient is asleep under general anesthesia.

In about 66 percent of the cases of early miscarriage the babies would not have developed perfectly if the pregnancy had continued. The woman who has had a spontaneous abortion has an 80 percent chance that her next pregnancy will be successful. If she has had two successive miscarriages, she still has a 75 percent chance of producing a healthy child. The success rate after three successive spontaneous abortions is about 50 to 70 percent. As you can see, the odds are that, even though a woman has lost one or more babies to miscarriage, it will not happen again.

When an infant is born after the twentieth week of gestation, or weighs more than 500 grams, and does not breathe or show other signs of life after birth, she is generally referred to as *stillborn*. Technically, any fetus who dies before birth is stillborn. In this book, however, the word stillborn will indicate a baby who died after the twentieth week of gestation.

As stated earlier, one or two out of every 100 babies are stillborn. Another way of saying it is that 98 to 99 percent of all babies who reach the twentieth week of gestation are born alive. If the cause of fetal death was not genetic, the parents have about a 95 percent chance of producing a healthy baby the next time.

Three myths surrounding miscarriage and stillbirth have been around for years:

1. *Accidents and emotional frights are common causes of miscarriage.* Spontaneous abortion is not usually associated with trauma, whether emotional or physical. Although many women who have miscarried can point to a distressing event or a recent fall, this rarely is found to be the actual cause of the abortion. Even abdominal surgery is fairly safe during pregnancy.

In 1913, Dr. Joseph DeLee, often called the "father of modern obstetrics," stated his belief that the automobile would someday be recognized as one of the greatest causes of spontaneous abortion. He was referring to everyday driving on bumpy roads, and without the springs that make modern cars so comfortable.

Actually, the greatest danger to the fetus in an automobile accident is the death of the mother. If a pregnant woman has an injury that results in severe bleeding, her baby may die from a lack of oxygen that normally would be supplied by the mother's blood. For this reason, and for her own safety, an expectant mother should use seat belts when riding in a car. It is important to use both an abdominal belt, pulled down around her hip area, and a shoulder harness. Studies have shown that, if she wears only the abdominal belt, the forceful forward motion of her upper body during a collision can cause the placenta to detach. This would lead to hemorrhage, greatly endangering her life and the baby's.

2. *Horse-back riding during pregnancy will cause a miscarriage or premature birth.* In his book, *Pregnancy, Birth and Family Planning,* Dr. Alan Guttmacher humorously points out that the type of activity a doctor tells his pregnant patients to avoid often is the kind which he himself does not enjoy or do

well. Except for scuba diving, sports which do not endanger the life of the mother are fine during a normal pregnancy. (Scuba diving is forbidden because of the danger that the fetus can be adversely affected by the pressure changes without the mother's knowledge.) If a woman is good at something and enjoys doing it, she should do it for as long as it feels good, unless she is having vaginal bleeding or cramps, or is placed on bedrest for some other complication.

3. *Babies born in the seventh month have a better chance of surviving than babies born in the eighth month.* This myth has absolutely no basis in fact. The longer the baby remains within the uterus, the greater are the chances for survival. This, of course, refers to babies born on or before the due date. Those born several weeks after the true due date may have difficulties.

There has been disagreement among medical professionals about what some call a myth and others a fact regarding miscarriage. Many doctors tell patients who are at risk of spontaneous abortion to avoid strenuous activity as well as sexual intercourse during the first three months of pregnancy at the times when they would ordinarily expect to be menstruating. In his previously mentioned book, Dr. Guttmacher writes that the advice to be extra careful during the eighth and twelfth weeks, when the period would be expected, is proven false by the statistics, which show that most miscarriages occur during the tenth and eleventh weeks. He continues by stating that "time-oriented restrictions are quite unnecessary."

The problem with this type of thinking is that the woman conceived two weeks before her period was due. This means that she would have expected her next periods to fall during the second, sixth and *tenth* weeks, not the eighth and twelfth weeks. In other words, there may be some validity to the precautions to take it easy and avoid intercourse, at least during the tenth and eleventh weeks if there is any doubt about the pregnancy.

To understand the process, causes, and prevention of miscarriage and stillbirth, it is necessary to review the normal course of pregnancy and birth.

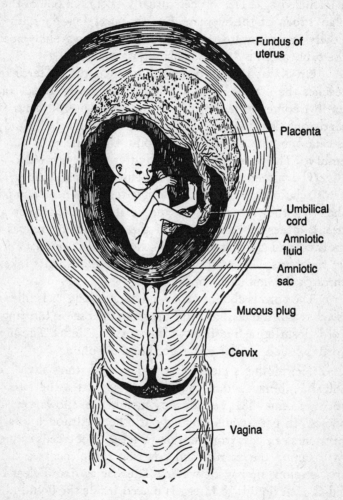

FIGURE 1-1. Fetus in utero.
Drawing by Jan Miertschin. From the book, Childbearing: A Guide for Pregnant Parents by Sherry Lynn Mims Jiménez © 1980 by Sherry Lynn Mims Jiménez. Published by Prentice-Hall, Inc., Englewood Cliffs, New Jersey 07632.

NORMAL PREGNANCY

Pregnancy begins when a sperm penetrates an ovum to produce a fertilized egg. This process usually occurs in one of the Fallopian tubes of the woman. For the next few days, the egg is slowly urged toward the waiting uterus by wavelike motions of the tube, aided by tiny hairs lining its walls.

On about the third day, the conceptus, or fertilized egg, reaches the uterine cavity where it floats freely for several days, until it comes to rest on a portion of the uterine wall. There it sends out tiny roots, securing itself to the mother's body. This is called implantation. At this point, the conceptus is called an embryo. The term "fetus" is used after the eighth week.

The placenta forms at the point of implantation. This organ's relationship to the developing fetus has been compared to that of a root system to its tree. It absorbs the oxygen and nutrients necessary for life from the surrounding tissues of the mother, and transfers to the mother's body the waste products of the fetus. The transport of these vital elements takes place through the umbilical cord.

The cord is about twenty one inches long. It is filled with a jellylike substance that helps prevent collapse or knotting of the cord, insuring a free flow of blood to the fetus. The umbilical cord is coiled, similar to the cord of a telephone.

The mother's blood never mixes with the baby's blood. A thin membrane within the placenta separates the two circulatory systems. The semiporous membrane allows certain substances to pass, while keeping out others. Although oxygen and nutrients can pass from mother to fetus, blood cells cannot.

Lining the uterus, and covering the placenta and cord, is the amnion, or bag of waters. This sac is like a clear balloon filled with liquid. If an egg is placed inside the liquid-filled balloon, it will be protected from breaking. If the balloon is bumped or jostled, the egg will not be harmed. In the same way the amniotic sac and its fluid protect the unborn child.

Besides protecting the baby from bumps and bruises, the

sac keeps her at an even temperature of 98.6 degrees. It supplies a certain amount of nourishment as the baby practices her sucking skills before the birth. The liquid also serves as a medium for the baby's movements. Without the fluid, the uterus would lose some of its shape, confining the baby's activities.

Perhaps the most important function of the bag of waters is that of preventing infection. It serves as a barrier against the outside world. Once the bag has broken or developed a leak, the baby loses this protection, making her susceptible to infection. The amniotic sac normally remains intact until just before or during labor.

During early pregnancy, the usually small cervix begins to thicken. This change insures that the cervix will not weaken under the pressure of the increasing weight of the baby. Several weeks before labor begins, a hormone called relaxin will start to soften the cervix, preparing it to thin and open for the birth.

Although the cervix remains tight throughout the normal pregnancy, a plug of mucous develops to seal the opening. As early labor contractions soften and open the cervix, this plug discharges into the birth canal. This is referred to as the *show*. It usually has a pink or brown tinge or may have threads of red blood in it.

In the beginning, the pregnant uterus will outgrow the developing fetus. During the first twenty weeks, the muscular sac increases in size by adding new cells to its structure. After the twentieth week of gestation, the uterine muscle stretches to accomodate the growing baby.

In the normal course of labor, the uterus contracts, that is, it tightens, pulling up and out on the softened cervix. This causes the cervix to be pulled up toward the body of the uterus, gradually disappearing altogether. This process is called *effacement*. Complete effacement is measured as 100 percent.

When effacement has reached about fifty percent, the cervix begins to open, or dilate. Dilatation is measured in centimeters, with ten centimeters being complete. Both dilatation and effacement can be assessed by a vaginal exam in which the examiner inserts two fingers into the birth canal and feels the size of the cervical opening and the thickness or length of the cervix.

As the uterus contracts, the blood flow to the placenta is reduced. During each contraction, the baby's heart rate will decrease. As the contracted uterus relaxes, the normal bloodflow is restored and the baby's heartbeat returns to its regular rate.

While the cervix is dilating, other progress is occurring. The baby drops slowly, almost unnoticed by the mother, closer to the birth canal. As she makes her way toward the vagina, the baby is turning to accomodate the shape of the mother's pelvis. This forward and downward progress is measured in terms of *station*. The baby starts out at a station of minus three or two or one, and travels downward toward zero station. At this point, the head, or the part that is closest to the birth canal—called the *presenting part*—is just at the cervix.

Through the combined pushing efforts of the mother's voluntary and involuntary muscles, the baby's head leaves the uterus and enters the birth canal, proceeding to a plus one station. Although methods of determining station differ, a plus three usually indicates that the head, or presenting part, is visible at the vaginal opening. This is called *crowning*.

As the mother's monumental efforts continue, the head emerges from the birth canal. The baby usually is born with her face toward her mother's back. After the head is born, she will turn to her side in order to allow the shoulders to duck under the mother's pubic bone. After that, she slips out with ease.

The pulsating umbilical cord follows the baby. Until it is clamped and cut, or until it stops pulsating, blood is still moving from the placenta to the baby, and the newborn is dependent on her mother's oxygen for life. Once the pulsating ceases, or the cord is severed, the child is on her own systems. The placenta follows the cord and is referred to as the *afterbirth*.

When the child is born, both parents eagerly await the first cry of new life. They stretch out their arms to touch and hold their baby. Even the delivery room staff watches and smiles in wonder at this miracle that never seems to grow old. Nothing can match the feeling of fulfillment and satisfaction that is felt in the room when it is filled with the first cries and smells of the newborn. Nothing is as soft and moist and alive as the wriggling child as she unfolds and folds again lying on her mother's abdomen. Nothing is as beautiful and adoring as the looks that pass between mother and father and child in those first moments of discovery.

And nothing is as empty as the void and the deafening silence when the doctor apologetically says, "I'm sorry. The baby is dead."

BIRTH WITHOUT JOY

CHAPTER

2

"I was in the bathtub when I had a strange feeling—sort of a pop. It reminded me of those body suits we used to wear and how the snaps would pop open. I felt some fluid coming out, so I got up to the commode to see if there was any blood. There wasn't, but I felt more fluid, so I told my husband to call the doctor.

"By the time we got to the hospital, my pad had some staining on it. The doctor said that my bag of waters had broken, but that my cervix was closed, so I was a threatened abortion. I remember I was worried about miscarrying and I didn't want to lose the baby. When he examined me I was trying to relax, and yet it was as if I was trying to hold on to the baby at the same time. It wasn't very comfortable. I felt afraid that I wouldn't lose the baby, and yet I was afraid that something would be wrong with the baby.

"I remember all these feelings going through my head, and

my husband wasn't in the room. He had gone to check on the children.

"The doctor sent me home and told me I probably would be back later that night. So we got in the car, but before we got out of the parking lot, I had a very hard contraction and felt a gush of fluid. I remember thinking how glad I was to have worn brown pants because fluid was leaking down my leg and running into my shoe. But at least the children wouldn't notice anything.

"The elevator ride was about ten years long. I really expected to see the baby when I undressed. I got on the table and the doctor got there and the baby came out. He said, 'You've lost the baby.' I cried a lot and shook all over, and in my legs quite severely.

"I asked the doctor if he saw anything wrong with the baby. It was like if there was something wrong it would be a justification for the miscarriage. But he said there was nothing wrong that he could see.

"I tried to do relaxation techniques, but I still felt like I needed to hold on to something. I worried that the IV would infiltrate, but the anesthesiologist told me to hold his hand, and he stayed there the whole time. There were eight or nine people in this tiny little examining room. I think all the interns decided to come down and watch and I remember there were so many people in there, but my husband was still outside."

Dana is a nurse and a childbirth educator. Her husband is a physician. But when they lost their third child after only four months of pregnancy, their feelings and experiences were similar to those of other couples who have had miscarriages. They were torn by conflicting emotions, while at the same time there was physical discomfort to endure. And, they were not able to be together when they really needed each other.

Dana went on to explain what happened after the baby was born:

"I felt sort of relieved as they took me to my room. At

least it was over, and I didn't have to wonder anymore if I would lose the baby.

"After my other children were born I had a boggy uterus, and had to have extra Pitocin. [Author's note: This drug was given to help the uterus contract and prevent hemorrhage.] I was so afraid this would happen again that I didn't take any medication or sleeping pills because I thought I would go to sleep and bleed to death. I wanted Mike to stay with me the whole time and he did, until four in the morning. We talked about how much better it would be without the baby, but it bothered me the next day, and for about two weeks I felt like I was going into a depression."

Fetal death occurs in a variety of ways and for a variety of reasons. But all have in common the combination of physical and emotional pain, along with fear and a sense of failure. This chapter will describe the experiences of several couples as they remember the actual miscarriage or stillbirth.

FETAL DEATH: CASE STUDIES

When Don and Virginia lost their baby, pain was one of the outstanding features of the experience. Virginia said, "I woke up early in the morning because I had very bad cramps, and then I noticed there was blood, so I thought I had started my period. After a couple of hours the cramps got so painful I could hardly move and I was losing a lot of blood."

Like many women, Virginia was not even aware she was pregnant until she miscarried.

When she and Don came to my childbirth classes for their third pregnancy, which resulted in their first live birth, their greatest fear was pain. They assumed that since the miscarriages had hurt so badly, the labor of a full-term pregnancy must be excruciating. A miscarriage is often more painful than a full-term birth. This may be because abortion is not a healthy function, rather it is a dysfunction. The contractions may be more like severe cramps or spasms than like the rhythmic, wavelike tightening and relaxation that occurs in a healthy labor. Often they are erratic and asymmetric, making it difficult to anticipate when the next will come or how it will feel. The fear that comes naturally when abortion threatens, added to the difficult nature of the labor, increases the woman's tension and pain, and probably draws out the process longer than is necessary in many cases.

Since most miscarriages occur in the first trimester, the couple usually has not been to a prenatal class or read books on pregnancy. Even those who are able to attend early pregnancy classes usually have not been taught the symptoms of possible miscarriage and how to cope.

The signs that an abortion may be occurring include contractions, vaginal bleeding, and possibly the expulsion of tissue from the vagina. Upon examination, the doctor usually will find that the cervix has begun to soften and open.

If a woman suspects she is having a miscarriage, she should try to collect and save all blood and tissue that is passed. She should immediately notify her doctor of her symptoms. She may be asked to report either to his office or to the hospital. When she arrives, the doctor will examine the tissue and ask the laboratory for a thorough analysis. If there is any question whether the woman has retained any of the products of conception: fetus, placenta, or amniotic sac, a D and C is done. Usually done under general anesthesia, instruments are used to dilate the cervix. The doctor then uses a curette to scrape out the inside of the uterus. This procedure is necessary to prevent infection or hemorrhage.

When a threatened abortion is suspected, but no tissue has been passed, the doctor usually will order bedrest for the woman. This often is carried out at home, but if the symptoms are severe or the woman has other complications, or if the situation seems to call for stiffer precautions, the woman may be admitted to the hospital. Sedatives may be prescribed in an attempt to prevent labor. Ritodrine, a new drug which was approved by the Food and Drug Administration (FDA) in late 1980, is sometimes used with success to stop the contractions. The couple may also be cautioned to abstain from having sexual intercourse, as orgasm leads to contractions of the uterus. Ordinarily, these contractions are harmless and do not induce labor, but under the circumstances of threatened abortion, it is believed to be a valid precaution.

(During her fifth pregnancy, Aggie, who had already lost three babies, had several bouts with threatened miscarriage, so her doctor cautioned her and her husband Allen to abstain from intercourse. Since he had not explained that he wanted Aggie to avoid orgasm, the couple practiced what they referred to as "outercourse," using other ways of showing their love and affection. This occasionally led to orgasm for Aggie and she continued to experience bouts with premature labor throughout her pregnancy. After their healthy son, Michael Allen, was six weeks old, the doctor told Aggie and her husband they could resume intercourse, commenting on how difficult the past few months of sexual famine must have been and how puzzled he was that, even with the avoidance of orgasm, it had been such a complicated pregnancy. Allen and Aggie's faces broke into mischievous grins as they explained their special form of "outercourse" techniques for achieving orgasm. After all, he had only forbidden *intercourse,* they added.)

Drugs to Prevent Abortion

Diethylstilbestrol, or D.E.S., was used in the past in an attempt to prevent spontaneous abortion in women at a high risk for losing a baby. Since then it has been shown to be related to problems with cancer in the offspring. There also is evidence that it may increase the daughter's chance of having a miscarriage when she becomes pregnant. Although there is considerable debate as to whether D.E.S. was actually effective in preventing miscarriages, some studies showed that it did not reduce the rate of spontaneous abortion.

If hormonal tests show the need, progesterone may be given to a woman with a diagnosis of threatened abortion. This management, too, is controversial and some research indicates that it is no more effective than no treatment at all.

If a baby is beyond the age of viability, but has not yet reached thirty-seven weeks gestation when labor starts, he is said to be premature. Five to ten percent of all live births are premature. These babies account for about two-thirds of all neonatal deaths, whether they succumb at birth, or a few days later.

Drugs that have been used with limited success in halting premature labor include intravenous alcohol, pregnenolone, and beta-adrenergics, such as isoxsuprine, ritodrine, diazoxide, and orciprenaline. Of these agents only ritodrine has been proven clinically safe and effective, but others are quite promising. Ritodrine is in use in many hospitals and some physicians send the woman home on the drug.

Even with promising new drugs it seems that if the uterus wants to contract, it will. So, is there really anything that is guaranteed to arrest a premature birth or a miscarriage? Dr. Neil Levine, an obstetrician practicing in Fort Worth, Texas, comments that doctors have a "chicken soup theory" of obstetrics. That is, bedrest will not hurt the mother and baby, and it just might help. He explains that, even if the treatment does not work and the mother loses the baby, at least the physician and the woman will feel that they had done all they could. That in itself is important.

Missed Abortion

Sometimes the fetus dies, but the woman does not go into labor. This is called a *missed abortion*. Judith told me that she experienced a missed abortion several years before, when therapeutic abortion was still illegal in her state. In the third month of pregnancy she suddenly did not feel pregnant any longer. Her breasts were not swollen and tender. Her abdomen was smaller.

Something felt wrong, and she was fairly certain of what it was. The obstetrician confirmed the diagnosis: her baby was dead. He told Judith to go home and wait for labor to start. When she asked him to do a D and C, he refused, stating that he did not do abortions. Judith asked other doctors to help her, but none would.

One month later, still carrying the dead fetus within her, Judith stood at the appointed corner until a long, dark car drove up. She got in and saw several other pregnant women sitting there. They were driven across the state line to a motel. No one spoke a word during the trip. When Judith arrived home, she had been relieved, at least physically, of her burden.

Today if a missed abortion is suspected due to cessation of growth and other symptoms of pregnancy, tests are done to determine the level of pregnancy hormones. The doctor will attempt to find the fetal heartbeat, and may do an ultrasound test to visualize the fetus and determine if it is still moving and what its size and shape are. If the diagnosis is unsure, it is best to wait several weeks and repeat some of the tests. In their textbook *Biological Principles and Modern Practice of Obstetrics,* J. P. Greenhill and E. Friedman recommend that the doctor wait for spontaneous labor to begin, because a D and C can be dangerous due to the likelihood of hemorrhage in these cases. They cite saline injection to induce abortion as the second best course. Some physicians are having success initiating labor by inserting a suppository of prostaglandins into the woman's vagina. This hormonal substance softens the cervix, encouraging labor to start. It not only stimulates the uterus to contract, but it also increases the motility of the intestines, resulting in severe diarrhea, cramping, and nausea. Medications are usually available to relieve the uncomfortable side effects.

A fetus which has been dead for a week or more will look macerated. That is, it will look as if it had been soaking in liquid for a long time and without the benefit of the protective oils and vernix caseosa that coats the living fetus. The skin will appear shriveled and shrunken over the entire body. Although some parents still want to see the baby, it is more difficult for them and the hospital staff to cope with this situation. It helps if the nurses prepare the woman and her husband for the baby's macerated appearance. (More information on helping the parents as they look at their stillborn infant can be found in Chapter 9.)

Sandra was seven-and-a-half months pregnant when her baby stopped moving. Her doctor told her he could find no heartbeat and sent her home to await what surely would be a prompt onset of labor. Six weeks later, she gave birth to her dead infant.

During those long weeks, Sandra went through the pain of answering questions from curious strangers everywhere she went. Seeing her obviously pregnant belly, they would ask, "When is your baby due?" To spare their feelings, she would answer, "Next month," and then she would hurry away. This desire to protect others is typical of people who have lost a baby. Added to the burden of their loss and grief is the fear of allowing others to embarrass themselves for having said the wrong thing.

Studies have shown that pain with a purpose is more readily tolerable and is actually less uncomfortable. For example, the soldier injured in war may not notice his pain until much later. It is believed that this is due to the significance of a combat injury: it means going home, or at least leaving the danger zone for a while. It also means a medal and an image as a hero in the eyes of the soldier's family and friends. This same phenomenon is one of the reasons for the success of prepared childbirth in reducing the pain of labor. Instead of bracing herself against the pain and suffering that the unprepared woman expects, the Lamaze-trained woman welcomes the working movements of her body, knowing that each contraction brings her closer to her baby.

Pain Without Meaning

The reverse situation occurs during a miscarriage or stillbirth. The pain is meaningless. It is another insult added to the injury of a lost baby. The woman cannot focus on giving birth, or be concerned about relaxing for the baby's sake. She just wants the whole thing to be finished. This attitudinal difference probably accounts for a great deal of the increased pain that many women notice during a labor in which the baby has died.

Some professionals believe that it is best to give the woman enough medication to make her sleep through the experience, so that she will not remember it. Others feel that she should have just enough drugs to make her comfortable, but not put her to sleep. After all, this experience is a part of her life. If she cannot remember it, she will never be able to face her loss, grieve over it, and go on with her life. Today, when so many obstetrical traditions are being questioned by lay and professional people alike, it is important to consider why the doctor or nurse might feel the need to give the woman enough drugs to make her sleep through the labor. Is it for the woman's comfort and benefit, or is it because it is too painful to walk into her room and see her grief? Is it easier to work with a silent, drugged patient than one who asks difficult questions?

Perhaps the best way to describe the actual experiences of miscarriage and stillbirth is through the eyes of the parents. Aggie and Allen had eight pregnancies and only three live births. Here Aggie talks about some of them:

"My first pregnancy was difficult to diagnose. I was four-and-a-half months along before the doctor was sure. Six weeks later we gave birth to our son. We never even got used to the idea of being pregnant, let alone being in labor or getting used to the idea of having a baby. He died almost immediately. Our biggest regret was that we didn't get to see the baby. It all happened too fast—knowing that we were pregnant, having the baby, losing the baby, not getting to see him. It was hard to identify him as part of our family—as a member of our family.

"I felt used, manipulated, ignored—no one listened to me

during or after the birth. The staff just didn't know what my needs were or how to meet them.

"With our second pregnancy, I was admitted at six weeks with hemorrhaging. The doctor did a D and C. The doctors would talk to each other and say, 'This has happened, and this happened . . . ,' but no one said anything to me about it. They told Allen what they *were going to do*, not *could* they do it.

"The obstetrician came to see me. I was feeling like a failure, not a whole woman. I told him how I felt manipulated and would have liked for them to talk to me and to have been considered more than just a patient. And, you know, he changed from that moment on. He talked more to people and explained things and he turned out to be one of the nicest obstetricians there. Everyone wanted to go to him. I felt like maybe it was because of what I said to him that day, though I'm sure other people had said it, but maybe I was just the dawning.

"Again, like the first time, I felt used and manipulated. I felt like a failure as a woman. If it wasn't for Allen's love and concern, I would have had some deep-seated problems. Allen made me feel loved and cared for. He made me feel like a woman.

"When the third pregnancy was diagnosed, we didn't get all excited—we thought maybe and maybe not. We went past six weeks and thought 'Yay! That's good! When we got past six months we thought, 'Hey, we're going all the way!' and we told our parents.

"I quit my teaching job, got myself ready, and fixed up the nursery. The doctor encouraged Lamaze. We thought, 'Hey, this is a way to control what's going on. This is a way to keep from being manipulated.' We thought that for a change we were really going to know what was going on. Instead of being on the outside looking in, we would be part of the whole event.

"When the baby was born, they held her up for me to see.

"Then suddenly they lowered her, cut the cord, and began running and working and mumbling over her. I saw them do everything they could for that baby, and I was glad that I was awake and aware enough to know how hard they worked on her. But, it's not man, and it's not medicine that determines the moment of birth and the moment of death. It's Someone Else.

"A priest came over and baptized the baby. They let my friend and my Lamaze teacher come in. (Allen was away on temporary duty (TDY) with the Navy.) The room was crowded with more people that shouldn't have been there, but they let them in for me.

"The doctor stitched me up and I kept remembering my baby's face. This time I wasn't quite as upset about losing our baby because I knew I did everything and gave her every chance I could and that the staff worked with me.

"Friends picked up my parents at the airport, brought flowers, took me home. The staff tried everything to help. The only empty bed other than in obstetrics was in geriatrics. They were very friendly, and anytime I wanted to I could walk to maternity and look in the nursery window and imagine I had a baby there.

"Word didn't get to Allen for a week because of security. He came home the day of the funeral. There had been an autopsy and we knew Laurie had died of a congenital heart defect. We knew why she had died. We knew it wasn't me, and that made a lot of difference.

"We marked her grave with a little plaque. The funeral was very important. There was a beginning, a middle, and an end to this one.

"Not long ago, I talked to somebody who had lost a baby, and I said, 'Love for a child means letting go. When the baby learns how to sit, you have to stop propping the pillows and let go so he can walk by himself. When he goes to school, you have to let go so he can develop. And when he's a teenager, you have to let go and when he marries, you have to let go.' I told her, 'Love is letting go. You love your child so much and you're having to let go now, when you don't want to. It's very hard.'

"And, she understood that. She knew she was doing her job as a mother by accepting her baby's death.

"After Laurie's funeral we packed her things. A lot of people have someone else do this. They don't want to see or touch the baby's clothes and things. But I needed to touch them. We packed them up and we cried and hugged each other, and we packed up some more. When we had put them all away, we looked at each other, and, even though we never said anything, the look in our eyes said, 'For the next one, if there is a next one.' "

AFTERMATH: PERSONAL

CHAPTER
3

"The first two days I was drugged.

"The third day, I cried all day.

"The fourth day, I threw the bed controls across the hospital room."

Susan was describing her feelings and the events that followed the stillbirth of her daughter, Ivy.

She continued, "My husband arranged for a friend of ours, a minister, to conduct the funeral service. Later, he told us, 'I have buried old people; I have buried sick people; I have never buried a newborn.'

"It was as though he didn't think a funeral was necessary, or appropriate. He said he had almost suggested that we not hold a service, but that, after he saw our feelings at the cemetery, he felt good about it.

"In filling out our tax return, I asked my husband, 'Did we have a baby or not?'

"We felt bad—as though we were trying to make money on it. But, it seemed that if we didn't claim Ivy, we would be denying her existence, like everyone else had done.

"The IRS wasn't sure what to do. After four phone calls, they finally said that, if there was a birth certificate, there was a baby. We called the doctor and he said that the fetal death certificate *is* the birth certificate. I guess that if someone dies, she must have lived.

"It's hard to have a normal conversation with my friends now. One friend—she's pregnant—is afraid to call or come over. I think she feels that seeing her will hurt me. Frankly, I'm not so sure that she should see *me*. It might make her worry more about her own baby. But, I do wish she would call.

"What really hurts is when people slip and think, 'Uh-oh. I'm tearing open that old wound.'

"I feel like I have to stitch *them* up."

A woman who gives birth to a dead baby faces all the physical sequelae of postpartum—the soreness of stitches and hemorrhoids, the constipation, and fatigue—but none of the joy. After Ivy was born, Susan said, "The awful irony is that my sister just had a baby. She's been trying to breastfeed, but just doesn't have enough milk. My breasts are so swollen with milk that they hurt. Milk is leaking all over. The nurses put a tight binder around me to help dry up the supply. It's just another painful reminder that my baby will never nurse at my breasts."

THE GRIEVING PROCESS

As with any loss, parents who have lost a baby must go through a grieving process before they can restore a sense of normality to their lives. The stages of grief are commonly identified as the five steps described by Elisabeth Kübler-Ross:

1. Denial
2. Anger
3. Bargaining
4. Depression
5. Acceptance

The rate at which an individual works through her grief depends on several factors, such as how close she felt to the unborn child. A woman who miscarries before she realizes she is pregnant usually feels less of a sense of loss than a woman who has felt the fetus moving within her. Expectant parents move through stages called "parental tasks of pregnancy." First identified by Reva Rubin, they include acceptance of the pregnancy in the first trimester, beginning to identify themselves as parents, and the child as a person, in midpregnancy, and preparing for the birth and homecoming of the child in late pregnancy. Adjusting to pregnancy is a slow, gradual process designed to give parents nine months in which to make the transition from adulthood to parenthood. When the process is abruptly interrupted, confusion results. Dana commented that she first had to overcome the momentum of the pregnancy before she could deal with her loss. Even several weeks after the miscarriage, she would hear a name on radio or television and think, "That would be a nice name for the baby," and then she would realize that she no longer had her baby.

In his short novel *Swimmer in the Secret Sea,* William Kotzwinkle writes a moving and poignant account of a young couple whose first child is stillborn. During their pregnancy, Diane and Johnny Laski, like most parents, had come to think of their baby as a real individual, not just a baby. On long walks through the forest, they had pretended they were swinging their child between them, and would think and talk of how it would be when they could do it for real.

The author describes Johnny Laski's reaction when the doctor tells him that the baby looks normal and that they should have no problem bearing a healthy child in the future:

Laski listened numbly. "He thinks that's what has been at stake, our wish for a child, any child, not this particular child who swung down the road between us. They can't know how special he is. They point to the future. But we're here, forever, now."

It is important to recognize that some parents become extremely attached to the baby in early pregnancy, and may feel as strong a sense of grief as a couple whose baby is stillborn after nine months of pregnancy. It is not for anyone else to say how much sadness a parent, or other family members, should feel at different points in the pregnancy.

The father usually is not as emotionally close to the unborn child as the mother. He was not physically pregnant, and this can make a big difference. Because the woman is aware of pregnancy twenty-four hours a day—feeling the baby kicking, the amniotic fluid sloshing, and her belly growing—she adjusts more readily to the reality of the child. To her, the fetus becomes a person sooner than it does for the father. He does not feel pregnant all of the time. He feels pregnant when his wife is with him, or when someone asks about the baby. The father usually spends far less time than his wife daydreaming about the baby and making plans for the nursery and layette. His main concern during the pregnancy is for the safety of his wife. He finds it difficult to relate to the child.

Although these differences can mean that the woman may feel a greater sense of loss than her husband, they also indicate that he may be confused at the vague kind of loss he does feel.

Richard and Cathy lost their first child after only eleven weeks of pregnancy. Richard commented, "Cathy thought she had been at fault for the loss. I was hard-pressed to find ways of explaining our mutual tragedy. How does a husband ever find the right thing to say to his wife when she has lost so much of herself? No husband ever will feel the joy of being physically pregnant, or the tragedy of losing the baby."

Another aspect of mourning that differs in husband and wife involves the woman's loss of a part of herself. A pregnant woman subconsciously sees her baby as part of herself. When she loses the unborn child, she mourns not only the potential son or daughter, but also a part of her own self-image. The father usually sees the experience as the loss of the future child, but the mother sees it as the loss of something that was real and present.

Because of these differences, each parent will go through the stages of grief at varying rates, and perhaps even in a different order. The father, who is not hospitalized or in physical discomfort, may progress more quickly than his wife. As a result, he may feel impatient with her, or she may feel that he is indifferent and uncaring. Many couples find that it helps to sit down together and talk about the pregnancy and birth, recalling step-by-step what they can of the experience. Although this can be a painful and tearful process, it is extremely therapeutic. The frequently-heard advice to "forget about it" can be damaging and can prevent the healthy mourning that is necessary for recovery.

Understanding the stages of grief and how they manifest themselves after a miscarriage or stillbirth will help the parents cope during this time of sorrow and stress.

Denial

"On Tuesday I didn't feel the baby move all day. I thought maybe he was sleeping. He didn't move on Wednesday either. On Thursday I went to the doctor's office for my regular appointment. He couldn't hear the baby's heartbeat.

"The doctor told me that the baby was dead. He said to go home and that labor would start within a few days. While I was waiting, and during the labor, I kept thinking he had made a mistake. Several times I asked the nurse to check for the heartbeat. She was nice enough to try, but she never found it.

"After the baby was born, I waited for him to cry. I begged the doctor to spank him to make him cry. It didn't help. My baby was dead."

Whenever we experience a loss of something or someone important to us, our immediate reaction is to deny it. This is a defense mechanism. It gives us some time between the actual loss and the necessity of accepting it as reality. It is nature's way of cushioning the blow.

It is important that the people around the grieving family not reinforce the denial by joining in the fantasy. Statements like, "Don't think about it," only serve to prolong this first stage of grief. On the other hand, trying to jolt them into reality can be quite harmful, too.

If one of the parents says, "There must be a mistake. Maybe it was someone else's baby," an appropriate response is, "I'm sorry. I know it hurts, but it is your baby."

The hospital personnel sometimes inadvertently prolong the denial stage of grief by giving the mother sedatives and tranquilizers. Although this is done with good intentions, it can slow down the entire process of learning to accept the loss. Unless the mother, or another family member, is hysterical, it usually is best to avoid drugs that can affect the person's mental state.

If, after several days, a family member still has not progressed beyond the stage of denial, professional counseling may be required. A nurse, doctor, or childbirth educator with expertise in this area would be a good starting point. Many hospitals employ social workers or psychologists for this kind of situation.

Anger

When the parents are able to face their loss, their reaction may be one of anger. They may say, "It's not fair! Why did it have to happen to my baby?" Notice the singular possessive pronoun *my*. Although both parents have lost their child, grief is private. Each parent views the loss as a personal affront. This natural self-oriented way of looking at grief can hamper their efforts to help each other.

The parents usually focus their anger on the people and objects near them. Susan threw the bed controls across her hospital room. Later, she was outraged at her family when they insisted that they dismantle the nursery, getting rid of the baby's clothes and furniture and toys before she returned from the hospital. Susan felt they were denying the existence of her baby. She wanted to exercise her prerogative as a mother to take care of these things, and she said so in no uncertain terms.

Frequently the target of anger is the hospital staff. Already feeling they have failed in their chosen task, the doctors and nurses may respond defensively. A common defense mechanism used by the staff is avoidance. This can have a serious effect on the guilt that the parents, especially the mother, feel.

Linda's baby died before labor began. She felt isolated—as though she did not belong in normal society. This isolation began in the hospital. After the birth, she was transferred to a general medical-surgical floor instead of the postpartum unit. The nurses there were unfamiliar with the physical and emotional needs of the postpartum woman. They knew even less about stillbirth. Although placing Linda on this floor had been a kind effort to keep her from hearing the crying babies and laughing visitors of the other new mothers, it just seemed to make things worse.

Not knowing how to help Linda, the staff carried out the essential care, such as making the bed, checking vital signs, and giving any ordered medications. Otherwise, they left Linda alone.

Linda's doctor did not visit her at all after the birth. He left word with the nurses that she should call his office in six weeks for a postpartum checkup.

I went to the hospital to see her the day after the birth. Linda had been dismissed that morning. The hospital routinely kept new mothers two or three days after the birth. She had not been there even twenty-four hours when she was shuffled out.

This avoidance behavior may cause the parents to focus their anger on the staff, accusing them of hiding all the facts. It is important that the doctor and nurses answer all questions as simply and completely as possible.

Writing in the *Journal of Obstetric, Gynecologic, and Neonatal Nursing* (July/August, 1977), Reverend Dennis Saylor, a hospital chaplain, suggests that those around the parents help them redirect the energy of their anger toward a more constructive purpose. For instance, they might join a group helping to fight the causes of miscarriage or stillbirth. Or they might work with a parent support group, helping others cope with their grief. Of course, this type of suggestion will be most effective when the parents have had a chance to work through some of their own grief.

Friends and family of the bereaved parents can help by recognizing their anger as a normal and healthy reaction, letting them know that they too would feel angry at such a loss.

Bargaining

When a baby is born alive but unhealthy, the parents may make deals. The mother might promise God that she will be a better person, or the father might vow to spend more time at home if the baby survives.

After a miscarriage or stillbirth, the bargaining is retrospective. Instead of saying, "I will...if...," they say, "If only ...."

Rebecca and Phil's pregnancy was unplanned. She had worked as a sales clerk throughout the pregnancy and had hoped to continue working after the birth. Rebecca never stated that she felt responsible for her baby's death, but she implied it. She said, "I guess it's just as well I had worked the whole time. I was so busy that there wasn't time to prepare for the baby. I hardly thought about the baby the whole time. I hadn't bought any clothes or diapers. We didn't even have a crib. At least I don't have to face a waiting nursery when I get home."

On the surface those may seem to be positive statements, but Rebecca was really accusing herself of not wanting the baby enough. She was saying that, if only she had been a better mother before the birth, she would have taken home a healthy baby after the birth.

Both mother and father examine their past actions to discover what went wrong. Because the mother was physically pregnant, she feels the greater burden of guilt. Often the father, not understanding what happened and needing an explanation, will unintentionally reinforce her guilt feelings by agreeing with her explanation of why things went wrong.

Linda and Susan both talked about how they worked all through the pregnancy, without slowing down as their mothers had cautioned. One mother mentioned that she did not really want the baby at first and that the miscarriage was God's way of punishing her. Donna had taken a long trip the week before her miscarriage, and she wondered if that was part of the problem.

Linda expressed her guilt feelings this way:

"Everywhere I go, I feel branded. I know it's silly, but it seems that everyone can look at me and tell I delivered a dead baby."

Because friends and family do not know what to say or how to act, they tend to avoid the grieving couple. This only serves to reinforce their feelings of guilt and isolation.

After a miscarriage or stillbirth, the parents have an overwhelming need to know what went wrong. Even if they discover that one or both parents may have inadvertently contributed to the problem, most of them would prefer to know. It is the only way they can put the past in appropriate perspective and look to the future.

If an autopsy is not suggested, the parents should insist on one. This will give a clearer picture as to the cause of death. In some cases, referral to a geneticist is necessary to discover whether there is a hereditary problem that may recur. When results of the autopsy and genetic tests return, most parents find that they were not at fault and that the problem is not likely to happen again in a subsequent pregnancy.

Laura sat in my office and gazed past me as she talked. Her voice was soft and passive, lacking in expression.

"I had planned on going back to work when the baby was six weeks old. She would have been two months old today, but I just don't have any desire to go back to work.

"All I want to do is cry. When my mother visits, I think how nice it would be if she would put her arms around me and hold me tight while I cry. I want to tell her about the baby and about the labor, but she won't let me. I can see the hurt in her eyes, so I just keep everything to myself."

Depression is a normal part of grief. In the case of a miscarriage or stillbirth, it may be compounded by the phenomenon of postpartum letdown.

Good parents nurture and care for their children until they are grown. These parents could not even give birth to this child alive. They feel like they have failed at the most basic function of parents. Even a couple who have other children feel a sense of utter failure and may lose confidence in themselves as parents. This serious loss of self-esteem is intensified if their efforts to recover some of the experience are thwarted.

They need to talk about the pregnancy, the labor, and the birth. Six weeks after the birth, Linda told me that I was the only one who would let her talk about the baby and the only one who did not tell her not to cry.

For many of these parents, there is an intense need to see the baby. They need to know there really is a child. They want to know if the child was deformed. (Even if this is the case, the images they conjure up in their minds usually are much worse than the reality.) Some parents want to touch and hold the baby. Most report that seeing the baby helped them a great deal.

I experienced something that helped me understand why these people have such an intense need to see their child. My grandfather died several years ago. At the time, I was vacationing with my family in Colorado—a trip we had planned for a long time. My grandfather's death was not a real surprise. He was an invalid and very weak. My family insisted that I stay and finish my vacation, but I could not. I had to return for his funeral. I knew that his death would never be a reality to me, and that I would always have a feeling of unfinished business, if I did not see him before he was buried. As painful as reality is, it enables us to put the past in order and continue living.

Laura and Ted's baby had been born with a cleft palate, a facial deformity. (His death was due to congenital heart abnormalities.) Laura did not want to see her son, and later she told me she was glad she had not seen him. Ted went to the hospital morgue to see the baby boy. He said it was difficult, but it was what he wanted and needed.

When Susan saw her daughter, Ivy, she said, "At first, Britt did not want me to see her, but I had to. Ivy lay there, looking like a beautiful, old-fashioned bisque doll, and I loved her. Every feature was perfect. I wanted to kiss her, but I was afraid her skin would feel cold. That would have taken away from my sense of peace at seeing her."

Recovery of their self-esteem is essential to lift these parents from their depression. If there are other children in the family, helping them cope with the loss will aid the mother and father in regaining confidence in themselves as parents. This also may be the right time to suggest that the parents get in touch with a peer support group. In some areas, parents who have experienced the loss of an infant are organized into groups to help other parents cope with this kind of tragedy.

There are two national support groups composed of parents who have lost babies due to miscarriage, stillbirth, or newborn death. They are Parents Experiencing Perinatal Death, P.O. Box 38445, Germantown, Tennessee, and SHARE, St. John's Hospital, 800 Carpenter, Springfield, Illinois. These groups are nonprofit, so be sure to enclose a self-addressed, stamped envelope when requesting information. Compassionate Friends, composed of parents who have lost children at any age, has chapters in many cities.

The grieving parents often feel that they will never again be happy or fulfilled. Friends tell them that having another baby will help them forget their loss. But they do not want another baby—they wanted *this* baby. The mothers often talk about feeling like there is a hole within them that nothing can fill. They say their arms "ache" to hold a baby.

During this depression stage of grief, the parents may experience physical problems, such as loss of appetite, insomnia, hyperventilation (tightness in the chest and throat, accompanied by shortness of breath and dizziness), and fatigue. They may sigh frequently, and may lose interest in their appearance. They also may isolate themselves from friends and family.

Studies have shown that depression frequently is connected to poor nutrition and lack of exercise. Although these parents certainly have sufficient cause for feeling depressed, it is likely that their loss of appetite and disinterest in their usual activities may prolong and intensify their depression. By eating well, especially including lots of protein in the diet, and exercising, even if it is just a daily walk, they can regain some of their sense of well-being. And when they start feeling better physically, they will start feeling better emotionally.

During this depression stage of grief, it is important that the friends and family support the mourning couple, letting them know that, although they have every reason to feel sad, they will not always feel this depressed and blue. Avoid telling them to "snap out of it," or "don't think about it." Tell them that you feel sad about their loss. They need to know that someone else also is mourning their child. Avoid saying, "I know just how you feel." You do not, and to suggest that you do belittles their own grief.

When faced with silence, we often feel uncomfortable. It makes us nervous, and it seems to get louder and louder until we just have to say something. Do not try to fill the silence with small talk and cheery conversation. Silence can be very important and meaningful. It can say, "I know you are not ready to talk, so I'll just sit with you. When you are ready, I'll be here."

Morbid curiosity is unwelcome and destructive, but do not feel you must avoid talking about the baby. It is okay to ask if it was a boy or a girl. It is all right to say, "Does the doctor know what caused the problem?"

One of the most effective and comforting forms of communication is touch. Laying a hand on a shoulder gives reassurance. Putting your arms around a grieving mother or father can help temporarily to fill the physical void created by the loss.

Acceptance

"Can you tell me the chances of finding a doctor who will allow my husband to be present during a Cesarean delivery?"

Susan had called me for help in planning her next childbirth. Her daughter, Ivy, had been delivered by Cesarean section after the staff had been unable to find the fetal heartbeat. Now, three months later, Susan and Britt were considering the possibility of trying again. As she put it, "We aren't really trying to become pregnant, but we're being very loose with the birth control. I guess that's sort of an unspoken decision."

Like many other couples who have lost a baby, Susan and Britt were thinking of finding a new doctor and a different hospital this time. She said, "I've had very angry feelings lately about my friend's baby. I feel angry and cheated. It seems so unfair that she has a baby and I don't. I'm also feeling upset with my doctor. Even though I know he did everything he could, I still wonder. I guess I'm feeling superstitious. It's like saying, 'You wore the green dress last time, so this time try the red one.' I just want everything to be different so maybe this time it will turn out different."

Although Susan's comments sound like a mixture of anger and bargaining, she has assimilated parts of each stage of grief in order to find an acceptable way to cope. This is an important step in learning to accept the reality and significance of her loss. She expressed it this way, "There have been a lot of negative feelings and, now that I'm starting to look for a doctor and a hospital that will support our goals, I feel I've taken the first positive step since Ivy was born."

PHASES OF BEREAVEMENT: ANOTHER VIEW

Glen W. Davidson, professor of psychiatry and chief of thanatology (the study of death and dying) at the Southern Illinois University School of Medicine in Springfield, Illinois, studied 1200 bereaved adults to identify how their lives were affected by their losses. For five years he also followed fifteen women who had lost what he calls a "wished-for child." This refers to a baby that dies before, during, or within 28 days of the birth. He found that, rather than passing through very definite stages of grief, they experienced a four-dimensional grief. Psychiatrists John Bowlby of Harvard University and C. Murray Parkes of London are credited with identifying what Davidson calls phases of bereavement. Although they sound very much like the stages previously discussed, they are far more flexible and descriptive.

Shock and Numbness

This correlates to the denial stage of grief, but Davidson's study found that these feelings peaked several times during the first few weeks, and again around the anniversary date of the loss. (The phenomenon of anniversaries is important when talking about grief. You may find yourself experiencing a great deal of confusion at these times. You may not even realize that you are measuring time according to the date of conception, the first visit to the doctor, the first time you felt the baby move, the expected due date, and the date of the baby's death.) These feelings of shock and numbness generally decline steadily following the anniversary of the baby's death.

During this time, Davidson found that the mourner is unaware of much of her environment. It is difficult to make decisions and to function in general. The bereaved might be subject to emotional outbursts at this time, as well.

Searching and Yearning

This phase of bereavement remains at a higher intensity for a longer period than any of the other phases. It is especially strong the first three months, followed by a gradual decline. Like shock and numbness, the feelings of searching and yearning peak strongly at the anniversary of the loss. Afterwards it decreases steadily, although it peaks slightly around the second anniversary. (In his monograph, *Death of the Wished-for Child*, Davidson mentions a random poll which asked how long a person should mourn the loss of a loved one. The average answer was between two days and two weeks. What he found to be reality was that it took about two weeks to complete the grieving process.)

Searching and yearning is characterized by increased sensitivity to the environment, anger, guilt, restlessness, impatience, and mixed emotions. Two mothers described to me their dreams during this time:

> I keep dreaming that my baby is lost and I'm searching for him, but I can't find him. I look all over the house and through the streets and I know he's there somewhere. I just can't find him.
>
> I have a dream where I can see my baby. He's with some other babies and they're inside a bubble. I can see him, but I can't get to him. It's like he's in another dimension.

Since this is the phase in which parents feel the most need to be active, it is a good time to consider joining a support group. This phase is much easier to go through if the parents have seen and touched the baby. This is the time when the physical loss is felt deeply. A woman will talk about how her arms ache to hold her baby and she may absent-mindedly feel her abdomen as though looking for the baby.

Some women become attached to a substitute baby at this time. This is especially true for those who did not see the child. Davidson suggests encouraging these women to find a substitute baby—perhaps a doll, or a piece of the baby's clothing, or a toy purchased for the expected child—and to hold it and imagine what it would have been like to hold the baby. To the observer it might seem that this is enforcing her denial of the situation. But perhaps it is a way of saying goodbye which can only be done if you have first said hello.

Disorientation

This feeling is strong the first week, dropping sharply after that. It then increases steadily and is very high from the fourth month to the sixth. Disorientation is on the decline by the seventh month, with only a slight peak at the first anniversary. The mourner may feel depressed, but she may try to make others think she is happy. Or she may take on a role of sickness, so that she can continue feeling bad without fear of criticism for not snapping out of it soon enough. She feels disorganized and still feels guilty about her loss, as well as her inability to recover from it like everyone thinks she should. She may lose her appetite and fail to care for herself physically.

Reorganization

Although this phase peaks in the first two weeks, it is very low thereafter and until the eighth month. It steadily rises from that point, and seems to be unaffected by the anniversary date, although it slips a little at the sixteenth month. By two years after the loss, reorganization is very high and continues to climb.

Now the mourner feels a sense of freedom and renewed vigor. She makes decisions and functions more easily. She is taking care of herself physically and has overcome the insomnia and lack of appetite. She remembers her loss and still wishes for the child, but it has taken its proper place in her memory and her life.

Not everyone reaches the reorganization phase. These people need professional help, and it is generally a good idea for the family to seek help together. Because the mother will be dependent on her family during some of the other phases of grief, they can help her to reach reorganization, or they can delay her.

Because some of the symptoms of grief are physical, and because parents who have lost babies mention a physical ache and emptiness, touch is vital to their recovery. It would be wise for the husband and wife to obtain a book or attend classes in relaxation utilizing touch and massage techniques. It is difficult to begin touching each other to offer solace, but if you are doing it for the purpose of relaxing, or if you are applying acupressure for the relief of a headache, it seems much easier. These techniques are easy to learn and fun to share.

In a workshop I gave for health professionals, the subject of the spiritual aspect of perinatal grief was introduced by one of the nurses. I was surprised at the overwhelming and positive interest the group expressed in this topic. We spent close to an hour discussing the pros and cons of spiritual support and guidance at this time. The consensus was that most people appreciate spiritual counseling during their bereavement. Many couples have commented that their faith pulled them through. Some have felt strengthened by it, while others said their faith was shaken. Many see this as a test of their faith. It is helpful for these people to read Isaiah 43:6: "When thou passest through the waters, I will be with thee; and through the rivers, they shall not overflow thee; when though walkest through the fire, thou shalt not be burned; neither shall the flame kindle upon thee."

If you have had an active prayer life, you know the sense of peace and relaxation that comes from prayer. Many men and women have told me that when they had trouble sleeping or otherwise functioning, they took ten to fifteen minutes out to meditate and pray. At the end of this time they felt renewed and capable of facing the world again.

In the opening of this chapter, Susan describes some of the events and feelings of the first few weeks after her daughter was born. She said, "On the fourth day, I threw the bed controls across the hospital room." At that point she had moved into the anger stage.

Like many people, she did not experience the stages of grief in their exact order. On day three, she had been depressed; this is the fourth stage, and had occurred before the second stage of anger. For a while, she and Britt moved back and forth from one stage to another. Frequently, each was in a different stage.

Susan's move into anger may have been delayed by the fact that Ivy was born by Cesarean section. The pain and the effects of pain-relieving drugs made it difficult for her to come to grips with her feelings.

As mentioned earlier, it is best to avoid sedating the grieving person. If, after several months, she is still in a deep, immobilizing depression, a physician might prescribe an antidepressant medication to help overcome this debilitating feeling.

Little is written about the difference in emotional impact between losing a baby before birth and losing one after birth, but I will venture an opinion. Neonatologists have noted that the parents of a sick infant will exhibit more signs of grief after the baby's death if they have been involved in his care. Some have seen this increase in crying and mourning as a reason to keep parents out of the neonatal intensive care unit, but most recognize it as what Klaus and Kennel refer to as "high mourning," which is generally indicative of healthy grieving. Since the parents who have lost a child before birth have had no chance to care for him, it would seem that this would hamper their mourning.

Some authors have described similarities in the reactions of parents who lose a baby to Sudden Infant Death Syndrome (SIDS), or crib death, and those whose child is stillborn. In each case, the death usually is totally unexpected and the sense of guilt is tremendous. Perhaps the greatest obstacle to recovery for the couple whose baby died before they had a chance to really know him is that there is no personality to mourn and miss. There are no memories.

Is there hope for these parents? Does the pain ever stop? Will their lives ever be normal again?

For most parents, there is an easing of grief after about six weeks. It can take as long as a year for them to complete their grieving, but they will always remember the baby—and the pain. My own mother-in-law lost her firstborn over forty years ago because of a knotted cord. She still remembers him on his birthday and lights a candle for his soul.

The following suggestions will help parents in dealing with their feelings and needs after the loss of their baby:

- Give each other plenty of love and support. Let this be a shared experience as much as possible.
- Find someone, other than your spouse, to whom you can talk without fear of judgment—someone who will listen but will not offer advice that may not be right for you.
- Let yourselves cry for a while, but allow yourself to hope.
- Take care of yourselves physically.
- Insulate yourselves with the love of a few close friends or relatives until you feel stronger.
- Be patient with yourself and each other. Do not try to resume all your usual activities before you are ready. Some work may be therapeutic, but too much will block out those important, but painful, thoughts that must be dealt with for a while.

• Find out exactly what caused the baby's death and whether there is a way to prevent its repetition.

• Do what *you* want to about funeral or memorial service arrangements. Do not let the hospital or your family pressure you into anything with which you feel uncomfortable.

• You may want to give the baby a name. This will give her a more definite and permanent place in your family and its history. Do not be afraid to use the baby's name when referring to her.

• When help is offered, take it. Give friends specific suggestions for ways they can help; for example, perhaps someone can drop off your laundry for you or bake a casserole. Or maybe you just need a willing listener.

Friends, families, and professionals can be a genuine boost for your morale and can speed your recovery. Use them—you know you would want them to use your strength if they were in a similar situation. Ultimately, though, only you can insure your return to a sense of normality and well-being. The loss of a baby is a tragic experience, but it is a rare opportunity for growth for both the individual and the couple.

AFTERMATH: THE FAMILY

CHAPTER

4

"I wasn't sure what to tell the children after the miscarriage. Our son is only two, so he hadn't fully comprehended the fact that a baby was on the way, but our daughter is four, and she understood. I didn't want to frighten or upset her, so I said that we had made a mistake and I hadn't been pregnant after all. There have been so many whispered conversations around our house that I feel pretty sure that she knows anyway."

Besides coping with their own personal loss, the grieving parents must help their children, their parents, and other relatives deal with the experience. At a time when their own self-esteem is at a low ebb, this may seem like an unfair demand on the couple, but the act of helping others work through their grief can be very therapeutic.

THE EFFECTS OF GRIEF

As with any tragedy, many parents describe the days following their loss as moving in slow motion and being out of sync. Some parents comment that it seemed that they were dreaming or watching everything on a movie screen. This sense of unreality is part of the protective stage of denial, and is easily recognized by anyone who has lost a loved one.

The mother and father may be caught up in their own thoughts, unaware of those around them. Pauline Seitz and Louise Warrick, writing in the *American Journal of Nursing*, November, 1974, describe one woman whose immediate reaction to the death of her unborn child was, "Why me?"

She felt guilty for not thinking first of the baby. She felt like a terrible person. Her baby had died, and yet her first thought was for herself.

After the funeral, the woman and her husband must deal with a continuing influx of phone calls inquiring about the baby, and with junk mail offering bronzed booties, diaper dunkers, and life insurance for the new parents and their baby. Parenting magazines ordered during the pregnancy keep appearing in the mailbox—a monthly reminder that they cannot hold and care for their child. (Susan made an interesting comment that reading those magazines gave her a reason to try again.)

During the days and weeks following the baby's death, the parents frequently find it extremely difficult to make decisions. They cling to the routine things of life, yet find that they don't come automatically as before. Some develop psychosomatic symptoms, such as tightness in the throat, a choking sensation, shortness of breath, sighing, fatigue, loss of appetite, insomnia, and irritability. Some will remain depressed for as long as a year. (Sigmund Freud once commented that, if we were not aware of the person's loss, the response to grief would seem like an illness.)

As is common after a death, the family may begin to idealize the dead baby. This is especially true in the case of miscarriage and stillbirth. After all, this child never wronged anyone, never kept his parents awake through the night, and never made any demands.

Reactions: The Other Children

These effects of grief on the parents have a tremendous impact on the other children in the family. The preschooler, whose fantasy world seems so real to him, may fear that his resentment of the coming baby resulted in its death. When he sees how hurt his parents are, the child's sense of guilt deepens. Unfortunately, children can have more difficulty than adults in expressing their feelings. They may, however, show signs, such as hitting a doll and saying that it killed the baby. They may show their concern by asking the same questions over and over: "Where is the baby? What happened to him? Why can't we see him?"

Some children begin to feel very insecure. They have lost a potential sibling, and now their parents seem incapable of handling routine tasks and decisions. The child may feel frightened for himself and may cling to his mother or father for safety. In many cases, the parents will overprotect the children. This is especially true of a baby born of a subsequent pregnancy.

Some children suddenly become models of good behavior. They feel somehow responsible for their parents' grief, and want to make it all better. Or they fear punishment for the death, and want to prove their own worthiness.

The effect of a stillbirth on the surviving twin can have long-lasting implications. Elvis Presley is one example. In several accounts of his life, Presley is described as talking with his dead twin brother, Jesse. Even as an adult he would ask Jesse for advice and would use him as a sort of sounding board. Because the dead baby often is idealized by the family, the twin feels a tremendous obligation to "make good."

The Mother's Reaction

The effect of having another baby too soon after the loss was impressed upon me by Sarah. At a meeting of bereaved parents she brought her new, month-old baby. Although she had planned on waiting until fully recovering from her first child's still-birth, she had inadvertently conceived three months later. Sarah sat with her infant in her lap. He was lying on her knees. She fingered him gingerly every once in a while, but could not bring herself to really touch and hold him. She said, "I'm afraid to love him." Tears filled her eyes as she explained her fear of losing this baby, combined with a feeling of disloyalty to the dead child if she did love this baby. "It would be like I had forgotten Sean if I fall in love with Jeffrey."

The mother seems especially vulnerable to a poor adjustment after losing a baby. She carried it inside her body and it was part of her. After a birth, new mothers go through a transition as they become accustomed to thinking of the infant as a person in his own right. Until then, the child is seen as an extension of herself. As the grieving mother goes through the normal process of internalizing, or taking into herself, a part of the dead person, she may make a comment that she feels dead inside. Ordinarily this internalization means that the relative takes on some aspect of the dead person's life or personality, such as when a son decides to take over his father's business, or a wife joins a crusade to which her husband had belonged. But, the unborn child had left no crusades, and no memories to internalize, so, where once the mother was full of new life, almost bursting to get out, now she feels empty and numb.

She may feel like a failure as a woman and may decide that she is unable to bear a healthy child. This can lead to a hasty decision for a tubal ligation, or the avoidance of intercourse. A woman may decide not to go home from the hospital right away, but may go instead to her parents' house. The family may suggest that she have some time alone to get over her grief. If there are other children, this is damaging to them and only increases their guilt ("Mommy doesn't come home because she is mad at me.") and fear ("Where is Mommy? Who will keep me safe?")

At first, bereaved parents can be blind to the strengths they possess. A friend, relative, or health professional may point out these assets in order to help them reestablish their sense of self-worth. Often the couple will complement each other. When the woman is feeling weak and helpless, her husband becomes strong, and when he is feeling defeated and depressed, she takes over. Even so, postpartum marital problems after a stillbirth or miscarriage are common. One partner, often the husband, may project guilt onto the other. The mother, unfortunately, may be only too eager to accept this burden.

HELPING THE PARENTS COPE

Writing in *The American Journal of Nursing* in 1962, Irene Mclenahan states that the family "must free themselves from the bondage of the dead baby." To do so, they first must come to terms with their loss. As described in the previous chapter, this is done through talking about the baby and the experience and about their feelings. Experts offer the following ideas to help the family face their loss and proceed normally through the grief process.

There is general agreement among authorities that the parents, and other family members who can cope with it, should be encouraged, though not coerced, to see and hold the baby. Although the hospital staff may balk at such a suggestion, fearing a response they cannot handle, parents who have seen and held their dead babies recover more quickly. Today more hospitals are aware of this benefit and are offering this opportunity to grieving parents. Of course, the parents must be prepared for a few differences in appearance when a child is not born alive, but these are usually minor. Due to circulatory differences, the baby will be more red than the parents expect. The skin may be peeling and the head will have more molding than usual. (Molding occurs during the birth process as the skull bones overlap to allow the baby to come through the mother's pelvis. It is the cause for the irregular shape of most newborns' heads and is a temporary condition in the normal baby.)

Upon seeing the child, most parents react just as any new mother or father. At first they just look. Then they begin to pick out familiar features: "He has your eyes." "She has your mother's hair." "His legs are long and skinny, just like yours." These responses are common, even if the baby had not reached the age of viability. If features can be seen, they will be compared to those of family members. This helps the family to identify the child as theirs—an integral part of their family. Just as these familiar features enhance the growth of love for a normal newborn, they help grieving parents bond with their infant.

The next step for most parents is touching the baby. Just like every new mother and father, they begin by using only the fingertips for some experimental touching. Gradually, they proceed to use both hands to explore the baby's body. If the child has been wrapped in a blanket, most parents will take this off to look at his entire body. All these actions are seen in parents of healthy children, as well, but in the case of a stillbirth, they become important to the parents as a way of assuring themselves that the child is normal, which is usually the case, or that at least the child looks human. Their biggest fear is that they have given birth to a monster. Even when the baby is deformed, seeing it will probably be easier for the parents than living with their thoughts of what the baby might look like.

Although the family may hesitate to ask, many want to dress the baby in the clothes that were prepared for his homecoming. Again, this helps them claim the child as their own. It might help to use items of clothing given by different family members, so that grandparents and siblings and aunts and uncles can be involved. In this way, the entire family acknowledges that they have lost a loved one. They join together in their grief and are better able to support one another.

The family should be involved in decisions about the child's burial. Although the hospital will arrange a "hospital burial," this is usually done in an unmarked or temporarily marked grave. That means that, after a time, the relatives will have no place to lay flowers. Because the marker is usually made of wood, it becomes impossible to read the name after a year or two. (Sometimes only a number is used on the marker.) In this case, if the family should later decide to move the baby's body to a family plot, there would be no proof of exactly which grave contains the right wooden coffin.

If possible, a funeral service and burial in a family plot will usually be the healthiest decision. Due to work or school, many families do not remain in the same locale, and for them the best decision might be a single cemetery plot with a permanent marker, or cremation. If there is a grave, a headstone with the baby's name engraved on it will be a source of comfort to the family. When Allen and Aggie lost their daughter at birth, they inscribed the following on the headstone:

> Laurie Anna Stryker
> May 4, 1971
>
> OUR LITTLE ANGEL

They had lost a previous baby, Shannon, after only six months of pregnancy. Due to a difficult diagnosis, Aggie was four-and-a-half months pregnant before anyone knew it. Shannon was born six weeks later. She said, "They asked to do an autopsy to study the baby. He died from hyaline membrane disease, and they said they were on the verge of a cure that would save other premature babies. We said yes, but we didn't realize that meant we wouldn't get to bury the baby or have a funeral service for him. There was no end to it. There was no beginning, no end, just the middle part. It was like reading a book in the middle and not knowing how it started or how it ended."

After Laurie's funeral, Aggie said, "The funeral was very important. There was a beginning, a middle, and an end to this one."

Although Shannon had no funeral, the chaplain arranged a memorial service, and that eased some of the pain and loss Aggie and Allen felt. If the mother is still hospitalized, a service can be held in the hospital. For many families, it is also important that the child be baptized. Some hospitals automatically contact the chaplain when a death occurs, but it may be up to the mother or father to request this.

It is important that the infant be named, so that he can become more of a real person. S. Bourne, writing on the psychological effects of stillbirth, called it a "nonevent." There is no tangible person to mourn. A name makes the baby more real and facilitates healthy mourning.

Many families treasure pictures of the flowers at the funeral and of the casket and gravesite, but they may hesitate to request a photo of the baby. Actually, a picture of the infant, even though he is not alive, can be a great comfort to the family and serves to strengthen their sense of the reality of the pregnancy, birth, and death.

Family members can help by participating in the funeral arrangements and service and by using the baby's name when speaking of him. This will let the parents know that the child was real to other people, and that others also feel a loss. (It is important that relatives and friends not show exaggerated signs of grief in the presence of the parents. This may cause the mother and father to feel guilty, and it also tends to belittle the parents' own claim to grief.)

RECOVERY

A frequently asked question is, "Will I ever feel happy again?" or "When does the hurting stop?" There are as many answers to this as there are types of grieving parents, but for most people, the first few weeks are filled with the pain and numbness of loss. About six weeks after the miscarriage or stillbirth, most men and women are well into their routine at work or in the household.

The parent who has other children at home to care for seems to recover more quickly, probably because he or she feels a sense of purpose and responsibility. The routine tasks, such as carpooling and PTA involve the fulltime parent once again in normal social activities.

Six months after the loss, the couple is able to recognize their own growth and to understand the earlier reactions of their friends. They realize that the family is disappointed, too, at the loss of a potential member, and they recognize that any lack of understanding or help was due more to ignorance of the problem than to lack of caring.

Unfortunately, some marriages do not survive the tragedy of losing a baby. Whether due to misplaced feelings of guilt and inadequacy, or inability to resolve their grief, many couples find themselves in deep marital difficulties afterwards. Grief is private and it causes us to withdraw into ourselves. This can break down the lines of communication, leading to further problems. When Neil and Judith experienced a spontaneous abortion, he told her, "I haven't lost a baby. You did." His inability to display his grief led Judith to feel bitter and alone. They were wise enough to seek professional counseling and were able, after much work, to deal with their differences.

Future children can also be affected by their parents' loss. Aggie and Allen are typical of couples who have had a series of miscarriages or stillbirths. When describing the effect on Keri, their daughter who followed a miscarriage and two stillbirths, Aggie said, "We were determined to let Keri know she had someone special in heaven—that she was not the first. We wanted her to know that, if we were a little hard on her and put pressure on her, it was because we wanted her so much and waited so long that we wanted her to be the perfect child. Sometimes I think we're too hard on her. The other day she came home from school with her report card and said, 'I know you want to be as proud of me as you would have been of Laurie, but I didn't get a good grade on my report card.' "

Aggie continued, "We were expecting a C or a D but, instead of Keri's usual straight A's, she had an A minus. Sometimes I think we expect too much of her because she is fulfilling all our hopes and dreams for the others, and because she is the first child we have raised. That alone is difficult."

AFTERMATH: SOCIAL INFLUENCES

CHAPTER

5

"What hurt most was what people said—'Don't worry about it. You can have another baby.' But, I knew *I* couldn't have another baby. This was my third try. They would say, 'Forget this. Put it out of your mind.' You *can't* forget it.

"The worst thing someone said was, 'Just be glad you didn't hold it, because once you do, you know it's yours.' That baby *was* mine. Laurie was a part of our family. To this day she is. She's in our family Bible. We have a mass said on her birthday.

"One of my aunts said, 'Well, when you become a mother . . . .' I *was* a mother. Anybody who has lost a child or had a stillborn baby wants to say, 'Hey, I was a mother. I really was.' "

COPING WITH LOSS

The actions and reactions of those close to the bereaved family have a profound effect on that family's ability to deal with their loss. If friends and relatives avoid talking about the baby and the circumstances surrounding the birth, the guilt and isolation of the parents is reinforced. But this is what usually happens when a baby dies. Our culture is only now beginning to deal realistically with death. (Or perhaps we are finally returning to a realistic view of death.) The loss of a loved one leaves us feeling empty and numb. It threatens us, too. It reminds us that we may be next.

To cope, or avoid coping, with death we hide it in hospitals and funeral parlors, concealing the body in ornately engraved boxes made of strong metal to give a sense of permanence and safekeeping. We are a death-denying society.

In many ways, we are also a birth-denying society. Most of us are born in a cold, imposing institution that resembles nothing in our natural living environment. It is a place that is sterile, not only free of germs, but emotions as well. Although pregnancy is a perfectly natural and normal biological function, the woman is treated like someone with an illness. Throughout the nine months of waiting, her belly is prodded and measured and listened to. Her body fluids are collected and examined. Her physical well-being is gauged and recorded by a myriad of modern electronic devices. Things are done to her and for her, but hardly ever *with* her. And rarely are she and the baby's father consulted as to their emotional state.

When the pregnant woman enters the hospital to give birth, she passes through the foreboding double doors with the words, *No Unauthorized Personnel Beyond This Point*. Her partner is made to wait outside while she is "prepped." Beyond the doors, the people in green take the woman's clothes from her, replacing them with an institutional gown of white cotton starch. The hierarchy is established. Caretakers wear green. Patients wear white.

The mother's jewelry, even her wedding ring, is removed, and in its place is strapped a plastic band listing her name and number, and the names of her doctor and hospital: she is theirs.

Yet, giving birth is the healthy consummation of a healthy and natural act. Indeed, it is unusual for an unhealthy woman to conceive. Still, procedures are done to her that even a sick person would resent. Her pubic hair is shaved, even though recent studies show that this increases the incidence of infection. She is made to empty her bowels by means of an enema, even though most women in early labor experience a natural diarrhea. Many women are attached to various machines during labor. There may be a belt around her abdomen or tubes placed through her vagina into the uterus to monitor the labor and the baby. An intravenous solution of glucose and water may be started, "just in case" of an emergency. Pitocin may be given to stimulate her labor and drugs to reduce the normal sensations of birth.

When the woman has been pushing long enough to just about push the baby out, she is moved to the delivery room and placed on her back on a hard table and her feet are propped up above the level of her head. (We are one of the few cultures in the world that forces our women to give birth while hanging from their heels.) When the doctor arrives, he probably will cut the lower wall of the vagina "just in case it tears," and may use forceps, furthering the surgical masquerade.

Of course, there are difficult labors that require expert help. Each of the above procedures has its place, but only in a small percentage of births. After all, we are not talking about an illness or an accident, but a normal occurrence. There are also excellent hospitals and birth centers where the staff treats the laboring couple with the respect and support due a new family. I do not mean to condemn all hospital births and to condone or advocate the home as the sole place of birth. Rather, my comments are intended to urge a reevaluation of our attitude towards birth.

When birth and death occurred at home, they were a natural part of the life cycle of a family. Today, both events have become completely separated from our daily lives, hidden behind the forbidding double doors. In stillbirth and miscarriage, the acts of birth and death are so closely interwoven that the ritual and secrecy become what several authors have described as a "conspiracy of silence."

Over and over couples who had miscarried told me of how guilty and frightened they felt until someone finally explained that spontaneous abortion is quite common. As Cathy and Richard said, "You don't realize how many other couples have had the same experience until it has happened to you."

ATTITUDE PROBLEMS

We just do not talk about miscarriage or stillbirth. The death of an infant—so young and unfulfilled—is unthinkable. And because we take birth out of the family's natural environment, the advice to "forget about it" when something goes wrong seems only natural. After all, this was not a real part of the couple's life. It was just an isolated incident, we tell ourselves.

Until we treat birth as a part of the "normal life cycle of a family," we will continue to add to the difficulty and pain of families who are grieving over the loss of their baby.

Perhaps the most unfortunate attitude is that of the doctor or nurse who tries to comfort the parents by saying that this is a "blessing in disguise." They call on the theory of the survival of the fittest, and urge the parents to find solace, even relief, in the fact that their child probably was not fit for life. This is a horrible thought, especially to the woman who carried the child. She begins to wonder if she had borne a monster of some sort, and becomes concerned about her future ability to give birth to a healthy child. Richard wondered not only what was wrong with the fetus, but "... what the Almighty had wanted to tell us. Was it that He saw us as unfit to be parents?"

"The most difficult thing to deal with is when my friends call to ask if I've had the baby yet. I hate to tell them he was stillborn—they seem embarrassed for having asked. It's so awkward. They don't know how to act or what to say. Most of them ask if I need anything, but they seldom call back."

Of course, people do not mean to be thoughtless or cruel, but, as one young woman said, "I just can't take it when someone else cries. I don't know what to say or do. It's very uncomfortable."

Unfortunately, this fear of being uncomfortable adds to the silence and loneliness surrounding the grieving parents. Although many couples express a desire for privacy during the first week or so, they appreciate brief phone calls or visits from close friends and family. They cannot deal easily with prolonged conversations in the beginning, but they need to know that others are thinking about them, feeling sorrow with them, and praying for them.

I called Tom and Linda several times after their son was stillborn. It was difficult to tell if my calls were welcome, or were seen as intrusions on their private grief. There was a great deal of uncomfortable silence. Somehow it is harder to wait quietly on the phone than it is in person. So much can be said with a look or a gesture, and this is missed on the telephone. Nevertheless, it is important to try.

SOCIAL LOSSES

A common complaint of bereaved mothers is that they have lost an entire set of social contacts that were established during the pregnancy. Expectant women tend to seek out other pregnant women or new mothers and to cultivate their friendship. They chat in the doctor's office and share experiences in childbirth preparation classes and they compare notes in prenatal exercise sessions. Their intention, not always spoken, is to continue their friendship, at least through those first few trying months of parenthood.

While gaining this new set of friends, many women let slide their relationships with single friends, or with those who have no children. Again, it is not really intentional, but they just do not seem to have as much in common anymore. Perhaps all her single friends work outside the home, or those who have no children and are not pregnant may be interested in different activities.

When the bereaved mother stops and looks around, she finds herself in a sort of societal limbo. She loses quite abruptly the companionships gained during the pregnancy. Friends who are expecting, or who have small children, are afraid to call or visit, thinking that their own fortune will serve as a reminder of her loss. In *Education and Counselling for Childbirth,* Sheila Kitzinger describes Kate, a woman who had been through childbirth preparation classes and had delivered a dead baby. Kate felt rejected by the other women in the class, and by her teacher as well. She was upset that, while other mothers were asked to come back and tell the group about their birth experiences, her teacher did not invite her to do so. It was as though her experience was not valid or important. Sure, her baby had died, but she had given birth, hadn't she?

Teachers and couples also find themselves in a quandary when it comes time to plan the postpartum get-together. They usually tell each other, "Look, let's not call them about the reunion. It would only remind them." As if they could forget!

Because the husband usually returns to work soon after the funeral, he may adjust more quickly than his wife. Men respond differently to pregnancy, anyway. They usually maintain the same ties of friendship as before the pregnancy, and do not go out of their way to develop relationships with other expectant fathers. There may also be a difference in people's attitudes towards the father whose baby died. Since he was not physically pregnant, his bodily presence does not necessarily serve as a constant reminder that the baby was lost.

Society frequently forces the role of "tower of strength" on the man, telling him to be strong for his wife, and let her lean on him. In doing so, we wrong him. I spoke with as many fathers as I did mothers, yet most men did not want to write or tape anything for me. They simply said words to this effect, "Just let the people know that it hurts us, and that sometimes we need to cry, too."

After the obligatory phone calls cease and the flow of condolence mail dwindles, the woman finds herself alone in her house. The phone does not ring. No one stops by on the way to lunch to ask her to join them, as they did before. Couples do not seek out the companionship of the bereaved parents. Social invitations do not come. Why does this occur? It probably is not intentional. Friends do not mean to cause further pain and isolation; in fact, they may feel that a dinner party invitation would be seen as a cruel gesture to parents who are in mourning. But, after a few weeks in their cocoon of private grief, the couple needs a gradual return to their former lifestyle. A quiet dinner for four in the home of friends probably will be welcomed by the couple.

As pointed out, conversation can be awkward. In *Swimmer in the Secret Sea,* Kotzwinkle describes a conversation between a bereaved mother and her hospital visitors:

> "You mustn't think about it anymore."
> "Tomorrow's another day."
> "Yes," said the girl. And then again, *"yes,"* softly.
> "That's right, dear. You should always look to the future."
> "What a pretty nightgown."
> "I got it at the K-mart."
> "They'll have the sales there now."
> "Everything will be half-price. After New Year's."

Not knowing what to say, the visitors tried to turn the girl's mind to a happier future and then quickly changed the subject. But all she could think was that tomorrow was another day, and it would probably feel just as bad as today.

Conversations can sometimes be thoughtlessly hurtful. Dana has two children. Her sister Ellen had tried for years to become pregnant. To their mutual delight, they both conceived in the same month. When Dana miscarried in the fourth month of her pregnancy, relatives murmured, "Well, at least it wasn't Ellen."

GIVING COMFORT

So what *do* you say to grief-stricken parents? Tell them how you feel. If you feel sorry or sad or confused, say so. Be willing to sit quietly and hold a hand, or put your arm around a shoulder. Just being there is important.

Bereaved parents comment on how difficult it is to re-establish social ties. It is as though their grief hangs like an invisible curtain between them and their friends. Those who take the initiative and talk about their loss find it easier to renew relationships, but they feel it is unfair and difficult for them to bear the burden of breaking the ice. It helps if, instead of tip toeing around the subject, you ask about the baby. Usually the parents want to tell someone about the labor, especially if they had used prepared childbirth. They need to tell what they saw and heard during the birth and to describe the baby's features and even their own reactions when they knew the baby was dead. Telling and retelling give validity and worth to the experience and are therapeutic for the parents.

For those who want to help the bereaved family, men and women who have lost a baby made the following suggestions:

Attend the funeral or memorial service.

In conversation, use the baby's name. (Notice in the opening of this chapter how Aggie's friends referred to her daughter Laurie as "it.")

Send a contribution in the child's name to a charity.

Donate a tree, library book or Bible, toys and other items for a church nursery or orphanage in the child's name.

Send a personal note, mentioning the child's name. (This is especially helpful because it is something tangible that can be kept and treasured.)

Take a casserole or cake to the family.

Offer to pick up some groceries or drop off some laundry or drive the older children to school.

Invite them to dinner or lunch. Don't just say, "Let's get together sometime." Choose a day and time, and then follow through.

Many of the problems described in Chapters Three and Four are partly due to the lack of societal support for both the pregnant family and the grieving family. Societal attitudes and changes start with people, and those who are nearest the couple can change some of these attitudes by their own actions.

SPONTANEOUS ABORTION

CHAPTER
6

Donna and Mike were surprised to discover she was pregnant again. Although Mike was happy about it, Donna found it hard to conceal her disappointment. Ironically, she had just begun a new career as a childbirth educator. With two active toddlers at home, she just was not ready for another baby—at least, not yet.

By the eighth week, Donna found herself beginning to look forward to the prospect of another child. By the tenth week, the enthusiasm of her husband and the excitement of the pregnant parents she worked with became contagious.

During the eleventh week of pregnancy, Donna noticed some dark brown blood when she went to the bathroom. The next morning she developed bright red bleeding and severe abdominal cramps. In the evening, after more bleeding, she passed several large clots. She finally passed a clot the size and shape of a shaggy, reddish-brown peach.

Donna was no longer pregnant.

POSSIBLE CAUSES

What causes a baby to be born before his time? Let us look at the type of women who are most likely to experience a spontaneous abortion. Dr. Alan Guttmacher and his colleagues studied the causes of abortion and concluded that the incidence of miscarriage was highest in women who are over thirty-five, have taken six months or longer to become pregnant, and have had a previous abortion. These women have a 40 percent chance of experiencing a spontaneous abortion.

The woman under the age of twenty-five who has conceived within three months of her first attempt, and who has never miscarried, has only a 4 percent chance of a spontaneous abortion.

Why do age and obstetrical history make such a big difference? In examining the causes of abortion, it is clear that many conditions related to age are detrimental to normal gestational development. Many of the obstetrical problems that contribute to abortion are more common with increasing age. Among these are uterine fibroid tumors, extensive cervical tears from a previous birth, major operations on the cervix, and aged ova.

Other causes include maternal infections, congenital abnormalities of the reproductive system of the mother, and defective germ (sperm, ova, or both) plasm. On the following pages we will discuss in detail the most common causes of spontaneous abortion.

Defective Germ Plasm

Probably three out of four abortions occur as a result of defective germ plasm. This is simply a defective seed. Whether it is the sperm or the ova that is faulty, the fertilized egg cannot develop properly and it ceases to live. It will be expelled within days or weeks of the cessation of development.

What accounts for defective seeds? In his book *Pregnancy, Birth and Family Planning,* Guttmacher describes an explanation given in a demonstration by Dr. George Streeter in a lecture before the New York Obstetrical Society: Dr. Streeter stood in front of the audience and took two pea pods from his pocket. As he began to shell them, he commented that, although he had no way of knowing for sure, he was fairly certain that the pods would contain at least one bad pea. Guttmacher continues to say that Dr. Streeter's guess was correct. One of the pods yielded a bad seed—a defective germ plasm.

There are many theories as to what causes a defective germ plasm. The following are among the most widely accepted:

1. *The egg or the sperm was old.* Radiation has been found to cause premature aging of the ova. The degree of effect is related to the length of time between exposure to radiation and ovulation. The longer the time span, the more aging will occur. This affects the ova more than the sperm because a woman is born with all the eggs she will ever have. A man develops sperm all throughout his reproductive life.

A conception that occurs at the end of the life cycle of the ova also seems to cause problems, again because the egg is old. Because of this, a couple trying to conceive might want to keep ovulation charts to determine when the woman is likely to ovulate. In this way, they can attempt fertilization at the beginning of the twenty-four hour life cycle of the ova.

2. *Either the sperm or the ova might have been inherently bad.* Nature is not perfect, and even a person who is the epitome of health will produce a number of defective sperm or eggs.

3. *There may have been a chromosomal abnormality.* Since the chromosomes are the basic pattern of fetal development, a missing, extra, or broken one can mean that the fetus cannot

develop in a way compatible with life. This occurs more often in women under the age of eighteen and over the age of forty. These chromosomal abnormalities which result in spontaneous abortion rarely repeat themselves.

4. *Fertilization may have been faulty.* Although the egg and sperm may have been healthy, normal development is impossible if their union was not perfect.

5. *The uterine environment may have been insufficient for continued development of a normally fertilized egg.* This is believed to be the reason that the IUD is an effective birth control device. It does not prevent conception. Rather, it sets up an internal uterine environment that is not conducive to implantation.

6. *Implantation may have occurred improperly.* Most eggs implant in the upper third of the uterus where the blood supply is the greatest and offers the best chance for proper nourishment and oxygenation. If the egg chooses to settle in the lower portion, it may not have enough vascularity for continued development.

A condition known as hydatidiform mole occurs when a defective ovum's circulation to the placenta deteriorates. There is no fetus present in these cases and the placenta resembles a large cluster of grapes. (The name hydatidiform comes from the Greek word for grape.)

In these women there will be a positive pregnancy test, but the uterus will grow more quickly than normal in about two-thirds of the cases. Around the fourth month, the placenta will begin to separate and the woman will experience uterine bleeding. She also may have nausea, weakness, and high blood pressure.

Parts of the mole may be expelled vaginally as in a spontaneous abortion, but usually a D and C is required to remove the entire placenta.

Hydatidiform mole is more common in older women and

occurs in about one out of every 2000 pregnancies. There is an 8 to 10 percent risk of malignancy. Women who have had a hydatidiform mole run a 36 percent risk of abortion in a subsequent pregnancy, as compared with a 15 to 20 percent risk in the average population.

Incompetent Cervix

Jaimie lost her first baby after five months of pregnancy. Her obstetrician found the cause to be an incompetent cervix. As previously mentioned, the cervix usually remains thick and closed until just before the onset of labor. If something has caused it to weaken, however, it may start dilating under the increasing weight of the baby. In this case, labor may start prematurely. This is referred to as an incompetent cervix. The condition may result from a previous surgery or trauma to the cervix, or may be a congenital weakness.

In the past, these women rarely were able to carry a pregnancy to term and deliver a healthy baby. Jaimie's doctor used a Shirodkar procedure on her early in the second pregnancy. This involved stitching a purse-string type suture around the cervix to prevent dilatation. Jaimie's pregnancy was carefully monitored so that, at the first sign of labor, the sutures could be removed and the cervix allowed to open for the birth.

When she was eight months along, Jaimie's bag of waters began to leak. The doctor admitted her to the hospital and removed the stitches. Although the baby would be a month early, he knew that labor would begin soon and the cervix might tear against the force of the contractions if the stitches were left in place.

The doctor told Jaimie he would check her later, but not to expect the birth for several hours or longer. Half an hour later the nurse called him to say that Jaimie was being taken to the delivery room. The doctor arrived just in time to deliver Jaimie's healthy six-pound baby girl.

Infections

An infection can bring about miscarriage in one or more of the following ways.

1. When a mother has an infection, the disease may be transmitted to the fetus. The unborn child may die as a direct result of the illness, or the infection may cause developmental abnormalities that are not compatible with life. Among the infections that may be fatal to the unborn child are syphilis, herpes simplex, and streptococcus.

2. Fever brought on by the infection can stimulate uterine contractions. Since high temperatures also may increase the oxygen requirements of the fetus and placenta, the contractions are doubly serious because they tend to reduce the uterine oxygen supply.

3. Certain serious illnesses decrease the mother's oxygen supply, which in turn reduces the baby's source of oxygen. Pneumonia is an example of this type of condition.

Before becoming pregnant, a woman should be tested for the presence of disease, especially venereal infections, so that she can be treated before conceiving. During pregnancy, any symptoms, such as fever, sore throat, persistent cough, diarrhea, rashes, persistent vomiting, or malodorous or irritating discharge should be reported to the physician so that he can decide if one of the antibiotics generally considered safe in pregnancy should be administered.

Other Maternal Illnesses

When a woman has a chronic problem, such as heart disease, diabetes, or kidney disease, she runs a greater risk of miscarriage. She also may have to make a decision about a therapeutic abortion. Either way, it is difficult. Before becoming pregnant, she should have a thorough examination by a competent physician. During the pregnancy she should be observed closely for complications. In Chapter Eight, we will discuss some of the preventive measures that can be taken.

Ectopic Pregnancy

Patti's period was already a few weeks late when she began experiencing morning sickness. Her breasts were tender and swollen, and she told her husband, Bob, that she was certain she was pregnant.

A few days later, she developed severe pains in the right lower abdomen and had occasional spells of dizziness and nausea. When Patti noticed vaginal bleeding, she asked Bob to call her doctor.

Upon examination, Patti was found to have a tubal pregnancy. The fertilized egg had lost its way and had implanted itself in the right Fallopian tube. Her doctor performed an emergency operation and, discovering that the tube had ruptured, he removed it.

Ectopic, or extrauterine, pregnancy occurs when a fertilized egg is implanted outside of the uterus. The most common site of ectopic implantation is within one of the Fallopian tubes, usually the right one. The rarest types of extrauterine pregnancy are those that occur within the abdominal cavity or one of the ovaries.

Ectopic implantation may result from structural abnormalities of the mother's reproductive system, infection that has caused scarring in the tubes, previous surgery, or tubal spasms. Recent studies have shown that women who have had an induced abortion are far more likely to experience a subsequent tubal pregnancy, as are women who become pregnant with an IUD in place.

Although several newspapers have reported abdominal pregnancies that resulted in live babies, it is extremely rare for an ectopic pregnancy to continue past the third month.

The greatest danger to the woman is hemorrhage. This bleeding results when, due to the increasing size of the embryo, the tube ruptures. The usual treatment for an ectopic pregnancy is surgical removal of the egg and its sac. In the case of a tubal pregnancy, the tube usually must be removed, as well.

Fewer than one-third of these women have a subsequent successful pregnancy. Many are unable to conceive at all. One in four of those who do will have another ectopic pregnancy.

Habitual Abortion

Perhaps the most tragic type of miscarriage is habitual, or recurrent, abortion. A woman who has three or four successive miscarriages is said to be a habitual aborter. Problems such as uterine abnormalities, hormonal insufficiency, tumors, and incompetent cervix have been associated with habitual abortion. In about 85 percent of these women no physical cause can be found.

Edward Mann, writing in *Modern Perspectives in Psycho-Obstetrics,* points to evidence that habitual abortion may be psychosomatic in *some* women. Recurrent spontaneous abortion is more common among women who are dependent, especially in their relationship with their mothers. They usually mature psychosexually at a slow rate. Often the woman's father is absent or is inadequate in his role. With professional counseling and therapy, about 80 percent of these women can carry a pregnancy to term.

Many women have expressed dismay at the fact that their physicians did not take their situations seriously until after the third miscarriage. There seems to be a belief that until the woman has miscarried three times in a row, there is little need for testing and diagnosis. These women also felt discouraged by the term "habitual aborter," as though it were something they were in the habit of doing, rather like a habitual criminal. For them the terminology added to their sense of guilt and failure.

Environmental Causes

Recent reports on miscarriages in women exposed to the chemical Dioxin have reminded us of the vulnerability of the unborn child. Only recently have studies revealed that this begins before conception. For example, one research team found that if either the mother or the father consumed more than 400 milligrams of caffeine daily before conception, there was an increased chance of spontaneous abortion. This indicates some effect on the sperm and egg before fertilization. Women whose mothers were given DES during their pregnancy are at a greater risk of miscarriage with their own pregnancies, indicating that the development of the ovum or the reproductive system may have been altered.

IUD-Induced Abortion

As previously mentioned, the IUD works by preventing implantation. Some people believe that this in itself is a form of abortion. Nevertheless, if a woman becomes pregnant with an IUD in place, and if implantation occurs, she has a 50 percent chance of miscarrying unless the IUD is removed within the first two months of gestation. Even then, her chances of carrying the baby to term are only 70 percent.

The Effect of Previous Induced Abortions

Recent studies have shown that the woman who has had two or more induced abortions runs a higher risk of miscarriage in a future pregnancy. Legal abortions are relatively new in this country, so the statistics are not complete, but there is a definite relationship between induced abortion and an increased risk of miscarriage.

There are other theories and reported causes of spontaneous abortion, but, in most cases, a woman may never know exactly what caused her to lose her baby in early pregnancy. And, in most cases, she will not repeat the tragedy.

STILLBIRTH

CHAPTER
7

"Allen was on TDY (temporary duty), so my Lamaze teacher agreed to coach my labor. A friend would go and help me in early labor until my teacher arrived. We had the support of our friends and the whole hospital staff. It was going to be really neat.

"Well, I went into labor early in the morning. My friend Alice came over and we timed contractions. My coach met me at the hospital and three contractions and a few pushes later, the baby's head was crowning. They took me to the delivery room and the baby was born.

"They held her up so I could see her, and then lowered her. They raised her again and lowered her. Then all of a sudden they cut the cord and there was a lot of mumble-jumble and running around. A pediatrician came in and asked, 'What medications has Mom had?"

"Nothing.'

"I was watching them. They did everything they could for that baby. My doctor came over and said, 'Aggie, I'm very, very sorry. Your little one has died and there's nothing we can do.'

"I looked at her. I looked at her very, very long. And, you know, Sherry, up until just a couple of years ago I could close my eyes, like I'm doing now, and I could see her face. But I can't see her face any longer."

What causes a baby to be stillborn? Although experts disagree, the major cause probably is maternal hemorrhage. Two conditions that can lead to bleeding are placenta previa and abruptio placenta.

PLACENTA PREVIA

Implantation usually occurs in the upper portion of the uterus. Here there is a rich supply of blood vessels to provide the oxygen and nutrients the growing fetus will need. Placenta previa means that this organ has attached itself to the lower portion of the uterus. It may grow to cover a portion or all of the cervical opening.

Because the lower portion of the uterus has less potential for nourishing the growing fetus, the placenta usually will have spread over a larger area of the inner uterine surface than is normal. There is a chance that the baby will not be as strong as he should be due to this lack of proper oxygenation and nourishment.

Placenta previa also increases the risk of infection due to the proximity of the placenta to the birth canal. There is a high incidence of premature births associated with placenta previa.

Although the condition may be diagnosed during pregnancy, it may remain undetected until labor starts. The major symptom is vaginal bleeding. As the cervix begins to soften and

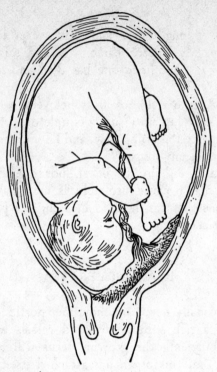

FIGURE 7-1. Placenta previa.
Drawing by Jan Miertschin.

open in late pregnancy, it pulls away from the attached placenta, causing bleeding. If the hemorrhage is not controlled in time, the mother and child both are in danger.

If the placenta covers only a portion of the cervix, and if the bleeding is not severe, a vaginal birth may be possible. If the placenta is blocking the cervical opening, or if severe hemorrhage is present, an emergency Cesarean delivery is performed.

The causes of placenta previa are not fully understood. In some women it may be due to the shape of the uterus. Recent studies have shown that women who smoke before pregnancy are more likely to have a low-lying placenta.

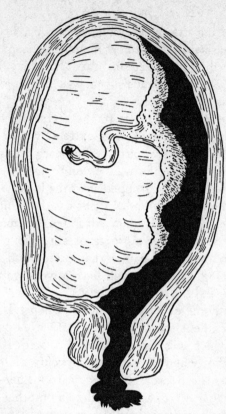

FIGURE 7-2. Placenta abruptio.
Drawing by Jan Miertschin.

ABRUPTIO PLACENTA

Bruce and Sally had completed their Lamaze classes and were eagerly awaiting the start of labor. They wanted to share this wonderful and challenging event from beginning to end. The end came on a Thursday morning.

Sally had developed regular contractions Wednesday night. When the contractions were about eight minutes apart, she felt a sudden stabbing pain in her abdomen. Her uterus became rigid, not relaxing between contractions. When Sally went to the bathroom, she noticed bright red bleeding coming from her vagina. Realizing that something was wrong, Bruce called the doctor, who asked them to meet him at the hospital.

The bleeding increased and early Thursday, before the sun had risen, Sally and Bruce's son was delivered by Cesarean section. He never breathed.

Abruptio placenta refers to the premature detachment of a portion of the placenta. (It is extremely rare for the entire organ to detach before birth.) This early separation of the placenta from the uterine wall usually causes severe bleeding. If the baby has already dropped into the lower pelvis, the head may block the exit of blood. In this case, the mother may not be aware she is hemorrhaging. Although she may not see any blood, there are other symptoms of abruptio placenta. These include sharp abdominal pain, a rigid uterus, and signs of shock. (A person going into shock will have a weak, rapid pulse; pale, clammy skin; and feelings of anxiety.)

The outcome of abruptio placenta depends on the extent of the detachment, the stage of fetal development, and the speed with which it is recognized and treated. If the woman is already in labor when the separation occurs, and if the bleeding is not severe, the doctor may decide to let her continue with the labor, trying for a vaginal birth. The mother and baby will be closely monitored for signs of further problems.

If the placental detachment is extensive, or if the hemorrhage cannot be controlled, an emergency Cesarean section is done for the sake of both mother and child.

If the mother is otherwise healthy, 99 percent of these babies will *not* die from abruptio placenta. Unfortunately, this condition is more common among pregnant women with high blood pressure. In these cases, the fetal death rate is 34 percent.

Possible Causes

The causes of abruptio placenta are not clear. There is some evidence that a folic acid deficiency may be associated with a higher incidence of abruptio.

Women with toxemia, or preeclampsia, have a high rate of abruptio, as do women with other conditions causing high blood pressure.

As mentioned in Chapter One, trauma can result in premature separation of the placenta. In labor, there are several situations that can result in an abruptio. Among these are the sudden release of a large amount of amniotic fluid. This causes the uterus to change its shape, resulting in the possibility of the placenta buckling off the side of the uterus.

In twin births, the delivery of the first baby may cause the placenta to detach before the second twin is born. Abruptio also may result from a physician's attempt to turn a baby into a good position for delivery.

If tension is placed on the umbilical cord, an abruptio may result. This can occur when a cord is very short or is looped around the fetus one or more times. As the baby moves down the birth canal, the cord is pulled taut. As he continues his descent, the cord may tear, or the placenta may detach.

FETAL HYPOXIA

Another major cause of stillbirth is referred to as fetal hypoxia, meaning a low oxygen supply, or fetal anoxia, meaning no oxygen is reaching the baby. It is difficult to distinguish the point at which a fetus goes from hypoxia to anoxia, and the terms are frequently used interchangeably. The two most common conditions leading to fetal hypoxia are placental insufficiency and umbilical cord problems.

Placental Insufficiency

Placental insufficiency means that the organ is not functioning efficiently enough to provide the fetus with the oxygen and nutrients needed to sustain life. Smoking, both before and during pregnancy, has been found to be a common cause of placental insufficiency. Nicotine is a vasoconstricter; that is, it causes blood vessels to constrict. When a pregnant woman smokes, the blood flow to the placenta is impaired. Smoking can create necrotic areas in the placenta. These "dead" places serve no purpose, and they decrease the effective surface area of the placenta.

If a woman plans on becoming pregnant, she should quit smoking several months before trying to conceive. If she is pregnant, she should stop smoking immediately. Even if a woman feels she cannot stop smoking completely, she can reduce the possibility of problems by decreasing the number of cigarettes she smokes, and smoking less of each one. It is a good idea to choose a brand low in nicotine.

Besides the harmful effect of nicotine, cigarettes contribute to fetal hypoxia by diluting the oxygen in the maternal and fetal bloodstreams with carbon monoxide, a poisonous gas. The expectant mother can provide her baby with vital oxygen if she will abstain from smoking for a few days before the birth. This will give the baby more strength to tolerate the rigors of birth.

Studies currently in progress indicate that "second-hand" smoke from other people's cigarettes may also have a harmful effect on the unborn child.

Other causes of placental insufficiency include poor nutrition, high blood pressure, hormonal insufficiency, and postmaturity of the fetus. This last condition occurs when the baby goes more than four weeks beyond the due date without being born. The placenta begins to age, decreasing its effectiveness. For this reason, many obstetricians will induce labor after the forty-third or forty-fourth week of gestation. Of course, it always is wise to obtain diagnostic proof that the baby actually is overdue, and that the problem is not one of faulty dates.

Umbilical Cord Problems

Maria was eighteen years old and living in Monterrey, Mexico, when her first child was born in 1938. When labor began, she was frightened, but since she was an orphan, she had no one but her husband to turn to for comfort. When she felt an urge to push, she realized that the birth was imminent and sent her husband for the doctor.

When he returned with the doctor, Maria was cradling her dead baby in her arms. He had been born with several loops of umbilical cord around his neck. Giving birth alone, Maria could not help her baby. As she told me this story, thirty-five years later, tears sparkled in her eyes.

Most parents fear that their baby will be born with the cord around her neck. Many mothers are cautioned not to raise their arms above their heads as this might cause the cord to wrap itself around the baby. Actually, nothing the woman does can cause or prevent a looped cord. About 25 percent of all babies are born with at least one loop of cord around their necks. Usually this is not a problem, unless the cord is so tight that blood cannot flow through, as in the case of a true knot. As mentioned earlier, a short cord may cause problems because of the tension placed on it during the birth.

In Maria's case, the cord was looped around the baby several times. This probably impaired the blood flow and also placed an extra strain on the cord. Had the doctor arrived in time, her story might have had a happy ending.

A serious situation arises when the umbilical cord prolapses, dropping into the birth canal ahead of the baby. This causes the baby's head or body to compress the cord, cutting off the blood flow. Doctors rarely induce a labor if the baby has not dropped, for fear that the force of the contractions and the amount of space between the baby and the birth canal, will allow the cord to prolapse. If a woman's bag of waters breaks with a gush of fluid, and if her baby has not dropped, she should assume a position with her hips higher than her abdomen. This can help prevent the possibility of prolapse. Although it is a rare condition, when it does happen, it is serious. An emergency Cesarean is done in order to prevent the baby from compressing the cord any further.

Other Causes of Hypoxia

Other causes of fetal hypoxia or anoxia include anesthesia (babies of anesthesiologists and others who work in the operating room have a higher incidence of hypoxia), dystocia (difficult labor), and breech position. In the latter case, it is possible to deliver the legs and trunk of the child, only to find that the head will not emerge, or will take some persuading. Unfortunately, due to pressure on the chest as it is born, the baby may breathe before the head is born. For this reason, many obstetricians perform an elective Cesarean on all mothers whose babies are breech.

OTHER CAUSES OF STILLBIRTH

Other, less common, causes of stillbirth include certain viral infections, drugs, radiation, maternal diabetes, birth injuries, fetal malformations, and erythroblastosis (Rh disease).

Rh Disease

It should be noted that, in most of the above-mentioned cases, the outlook is good. For example, recent advances have almost eliminated erythroblastosis as a cause of fetal death. This condition can occur when a woman with Rh negative blood conceives the child of a man with Rh positive blood. If the baby's blood is positive, in other words, it contains the Rh factor, the mother's blood may produce antibodies against it. Ordinarily, the maternal and fetal blood do not mix, but during a previous birth, or an amniocentesis, or if there has been physical trauma, this may happen. If the Rh positive blood enters her bloodstream, her body will react to it as a foreign body and form antibodies to kill it.

Although blood does not pass through the placental barrier, the antibodies do. Even so, there is usually little chance of enough antibodies building up to affect the child during whose gestation the first exposure occurs. But, in a subsequent pregnancy, there is enough time for the antibodies to build and destroy the baby's blood.

Any Rh negative woman should always receive an injection of RhoGam after each birth of an Rh positive baby and after each miscarriage. Given within seventy-two hours of each of the above occurrences, RhoGam confers almost complete protection to the woman's future babies. If the amount of blood that mixed was great, or if immunization is delayed, the woman can be monitored in future pregnancies. If antibody levels rise to a dangerous level, the baby can be given an exchange blood transfusion while inside the womb. Mothers who, for some reason, already have a high level of Rh antibodies, and for whom fetal transfusion is not indicated, have been treated with high level anti-Rh plasma with great success. One study, reported in the *Medical Tribune* in February, 1981, described the administration of 3000 doses with only four failures. (This research was done at St. Mary's Health Center in St. Louis, Missouri.)

In cases of hemorrhage or hypoxia, the fetus will show signs of distress that can be detected with a stethoscope or fetal monitor. If it appears that the fetus cannot tolerate the situation, an emergency Cesarean often will save the baby.

Although it seems that there are so many potential dangers that it is a wonder any babies survive birth, the ratio of problem births to healthy babies is quite low. Many of the causes of stillbirth are related. For instance, placenta previa or abruptio placenta can lead to hypoxia, as well as hemorrhage. As stated in Chapter One, 98 to 99 percent of all babies who make it past the age of viability are born alive. If yours was not in this number, perhaps knowing some of the causes has helped you understand. It may even help you prevent problems in another pregnancy. If knowing these facts has made you feel guilty, remember that most cases of stillbirth are accidental and do not repeat themselves in a subsequent pregnancy.

Parents often ask me how often a husband will be requested to make a decision during labor to save either the mother or the baby. I cannot think of a situation that would call for such a decision, other than if the mother has undergone severe physical trauma, as in a catastrophic accident. I have not heard of this happening to any of the almost 5000 pregnant people I have worked with over the years. (I do notice that it happens with regularity on television dramas!)

In early pregnancy, if the mother has a medical condition that causes the pregnancy to threaten her life, a therapeutic abortion may be recommended. In these cases, if she decides to maintain the pregnancy, both she and the baby may be in danger. Any condition that threatens the mother threatens the unborn child.

One question has not been answered here and is often implied, but never asked: "Is it ever the doctor's fault?" Before answering that question, we must weigh two important considerations:

• The physician deals with the most unpredictable product of all: the human body. The obstetrician has to cope with two of these humans, and one she cannot touch—she cannot even see. From most professionals we ask their best effort. If these efforts are not enough, we accept this as an example of our own frailty as human beings. We rarely offer this forgiving attitude to our doctor.

• In our search for a technically perfect birth, we have recently realized that the human experience may be missing. We must be extremely thoughtful about just how far we want technology to intrude into our lives. If we insist on a perfect product, and if we hold our doctor responsible for failure, then it is natural for him to react by using all the technology at hand. What we must decide is whether the price in loss of dignity and the strain on the couple's relationship and the woman's sense of her own self-value is worth it.

THE EFFECT OF MEDICATIONS

In looking at medicine and fetal death, it is interesting first to note some of the historical causes, as well as the myths surrounding the problem. In the quest for a perfect drug to initiate labor, researchers have found that it is often the patient who pays the price when we try to outsmart nature.

In *Women As Mothers*, noted British anthropologist Sheila Kitzinger, describes the use of ergot to accelerate labors in 1808. The physician who worked with this drug claimed that he had "rarely . . . been detained more than three hours." He was obviously proud of the way in which he had shortened labors for so many women, not to mention himself. But within several years it was noticed that the rate of stillbirths had dramatically increased. Kitzinger reports that ergot went from being called "pulvis ad partum" (powder for birth) to "pulvis ad mortem" (powder for death).

Still doctors sought ways to initiate and augment labor. In the early 1900s repeated doses of quinine were used. The fetal death rate from this procedure was 5 percent.

Today Pitocin, a synthetic form of oxytocin, is commonly used to bring on contractions or to stimulate a sluggish labor. Some of the complications of this practice include uterine tetany (prolonged contractions), abruptio placenta, fetal distress, and stillbirth. An induced labor may also be associated with prolonged labor, prolapsed cord, pelvic infection, and prematurity, a major cause of neonatal death.

Obviously, some labors must be artificially aided. The answer to the problem seems to lie in the careful selection of those patients, including fetus as well as mother, to be induced. Dr. E. H. Bishop has devised a scoring system involving the evaluation of several factors, including dilatation, effacement, station, consistency of the cervix, and position of the cervix. When using this system to assess candidates for induction and augmentation, along with ensuring that the uterus relaxes well between contractions, doctors have found the rate of complications to decrease.

Besides using a scoring system to evaluate the mother's readiness for induction, it is imperative that tests for fetal maturity be done as well. There can be no excuse for delivering a premature baby by means of induction, unless there are medical complications that far outweigh the potential problems for the child.

MYTHS

The myths surrounding both miscarriage and stillbirth are legion, and many continue even today. In fourteenth century, medieval Europe, stillbirths were believed to be caused by the midwife. During the Inquisition, Pope Innocent III declared these women to be witches. They were thought to use their single long fingernail, ordinarily employed in rupturing the amniotic sac, to puncture the fontanel, or soft spot, on the baby's head, killing him before he could be baptized.

Dr. Joseph B. DeLee, the "father of modern obstetrics," wrote in 1913: "Sea-bathing is adopted by some women to bring on abortion." He strongly cautioned patients to avoid the sea if they wished to continue their pregnancies. He also cited intercourse as a cause of miscarriage, explaining that the impact of the penis on the cervix and the resultant pelvic congestion would bring on labor. DeLee referred to the fact that animals do not copulate during pregnancy, and he furthered his stand by stating that some cultures and religions absolutely forbid intercourse with a pregnant woman.

Many couples have worried about the supposed dangers of intercourse during pregnancy. As long as there are no problems, that is, the woman has had no vaginal bleeding or abdominal pain or threatened miscarriage, and the bag of waters is intact, intercourse is safe. Coitus has been used by many couples throughout the years to bring on an overdue labor. They have found that, unless it is time, the uterus just will not cooperate. It can be, however, an enjoyable way to pass the time while waiting. Indeed, some cultures encourage coitus during labor to stimulate contractions and relieve pain.

Dr. DeLee was also concerned about baths. He commented that hot and cold baths, as well as steam and sitz baths, would excite uterine contractions, possibly bringing spontaneous abortion. Although these beliefs have been disproven, it is currently thought that very hot temperatures, such as in steam baths, whirlpools, and hot tubs may be detrimental to the developing fetus. At this point, research is inconclusive.

One of DeLee's patients was frightened by a fire and later aborted. The fetus was tangled in the umbilical cord, which also had a true knot. Another woman was frightened during a thunderstorm. The child's movements became violent and then stopped. A week later she delivered a dead baby. These observations led the doctor to the conclusion, "That great mental excitement can produce abortion is a daily experience." With controlled studies, we now know that this is untrue. Prolonged stress can be harmful, but a single incident of fright or stress is unlikely to cause abortion.

So what about today's doctor? Does he ever contribute to the cause of fetal death? Almost always he has done everything in his power to keep the pregnancy healthy. Sometimes his attempts go awry. For example, in the past ten years we have learned a great deal about prenatal nutrition. Studies show that the woman needs to gain about twenty-five or thirty pounds to provide her baby with the optimum health. This usually means an intake of 2000 to 3000 calories daily. Yet there are many doctors who place pregnant women on 1000 calorie diets. They scold their patients for gaining four pounds in a month and try to hold them to a twenty pound or less weight gain. If the fetus is healthy in other aspects, this malnutrition may not do permanent damage, but a vulnerable baby could be in danger of her life.

Many women who smoke heavily have told me that their doctors said quitting cigarettes during pregnancy would be too stressful so they continued smoking several packs daily, to the detriment of their babies.

These are ways in which the doctor's failure to use his role as educator can harm the mother and her unborn child. There are also sins of commission. Recently the CBS magazine *Sixty Minutes* profiled a surgeon who operated on a woman for uterine fibroid tumors, and found instead a five-month fetus. There have been other cases where a doctor did not perform a pregnancy test before surgery. This is not always fatal to the child, if the work is not being done on the uterus. But the effects of anesthesia and surgery increase the risk of abortion.

Sometimes the problem is one of waiting too long. The woman calls on Saturday night and says her bag of waters is leaking. Since she is feeling no contractions, the doctor tells her to wait until they start or to come in on Monday. By then infection has overtaken the baby, and perhaps the mother.

Or the doctor keeps trying for a vaginal delivery, when the baby needs a Cesarean birth. This is probably the exception today, and I do not want to encourage a quick knife. But it does happen.

Most of the time, everyone—doctors, nurses, and parents—did everything they could. It just was not enough. Susan's testimony was one I heard often: "If it hadn't been for my doctor, I wouldn't have made it. He stayed with me all night trying to figure out what to do. But in the end, there was just nothing anyone could do."

CAN WE HAVE
A HEALTHY BABY?

CHAPTER

8

"I've lost seven babies—most after only a few months of pregnancy. But, I carried the last two for seven months before losing them. This time the doctor put me in the hospital when I was six months along. He says he'll do a Cesarean section when the baby is about thirty-six or thirty-eight weeks."

The thin, young woman could not have been older than twenty-three or twenty-four. Anne had developed diabetes as a teenager. The disease had cost her seven babies, and now it threatened the life of her eighth child. Anne's husband had to stay behind in the little town where he worked as a crewman on an oil rig. He was able to visit her every other weekend. The emotional wear and tear was beginning to show on both of them, but even after the strain of losing seven babies, and after almost two months in the hospital, Anne had hope that this time she would take home a healthy infant—and two weeks later, she did.

Eighty percent of the women who have had one miscarriage will give birth to a healthy baby the next time. Even after several miscarriages, the odds are that she will be successful in a subsequent pregnancy. These figures are the result of the "accidental" causes of most spontaneous abortions. When Steve and Robin lost their first baby after only ten weeks of pregnancy, they were visibly shaken. Robin said, "The doctor told us it was a defective egg. That really scares me. We don't even know if we should try again."

Unfortunately, her doctor had given Robin a diagnosis without an explanation. I was able to assure her that what happened was an unfortunate accident, and that it was extremely unlikely that it would recur. The same is true of most other causes of miscarriage and stillbirth, such as placenta previa, abruptio placenta, umbilical cord accidents, and malpresentations.

PREVENTION AND TREATMENT

Progress is also being made in preventing and/or treating the causes of fetal death and loss. Measures include preconceptual examination and counseling or treatment, careful prenatal screening and care, as well as expert monitoring and intervention in labor and delivery.

This chapter will describe current preventive measures, as well as some of those still in the research and development stage. Many of these techniques are used routinely in all pregnancies. Others are reserved for high-risk cases. The following criteria are used to determine whether a woman falls in the category of low, moderate, or high-risk for problems during pregnancy and birth.

CRITERIA FOR DETERMINING RISKS

Age

Women at either end of the childbearing spectrum have a greater potential for problems than those in the middle years. Teenagers run a higher risk of toxemia during pregnancy and abnormal uterine activity during labor and delivery.

Older women have a greater tendency toward high blood pressure. They also may have developed physical problems in a previous childbirth which will give them trouble now. The older woman expecting her first child may have had difficulty conceiving, a sign that she might have a structural, hormonal, or other reproductive problem. She may also have narrowed uterine blood vessels, which would mean a poor blood supply to the placenta, and her uterus itself may be fibrous, leading to less stretchability and inefficient contractions during labor.

Parity

This term refers to how many times a woman has given birth to a baby past twenty-eight weeks gestation. Although a woman who has never given birth is actually a nullipara ("no births"), she is commonly referred to as a *primipara,* meaning this is her first birth. The slang term for primipara is "primip." A woman who has had more than one birth is a *multipara,* or multip. This is also used to describe the woman who has given birth only once, but is pregnant again.

Gravida refers to how many times a woman has been pregnant. A *nulligravida* is not, and has never been, pregnant. A *primigravida* is in her first pregnancy. A *multigravida* has had more than one pregnancy.

The parity of a woman can make some difference in her potential for problems. For example, the primip is more prone to toxemia. She also has never proven that her pelvis is large enough to give birth, or that her uterus will effectively dilate and efface. With the primip there are more unknowns than with the experienced mother.

The multip who has had five or more babies, called a "grand multip," also runs a higher risk. She may suffer from anemia, fatigue, and general poor health. High blood pressure and diabetes are also more common in these women.

Obstetrical History

If a woman has experienced a previous loss during pregnancy or birth, there is a greater chance of a future loss. Certain conditions, such as placenta previa or prolapsed cord, are not likely to repeat themselves, but fetal loss due to diabetes or high blood pressure signals possible danger in subsequent pregnancies.

Family History

If the family history of either the woman or her husband includes a genetic or hereditary defect, there is a chance of the fetus developing the problem. (Studies have not shown that a family history of difficult pregnancies or labors has any bearing.)

Pelvis

Any structural abnormalities may cause problems, especially in labor and delivery.

Medical History

Diabetes, hyperthyroidism, hypertension, kidney or heart disease, and other chronic illnesses can have a detrimental effect on childbearing. If a woman is taking a drug for a medical condition, this, too, must be considered, as it may be harmful to the fetus. (She should discontinue such medications only with the consent of her physician.)

Weight

A woman who is either underweight or overweight has a greater potential for problems than does the woman of average weight.

Emotional Status and Support Systems

Lack of positive emotional and social support can have a deleterious effect on the woman's health and on her adjustment to pregnancy. Studies have shown a connection between the pregnant woman's emotional state and complicated pregnancy.

Complications

As the pregnancy progresses, a complication, such as Rh incompatibility, toxemia, or gestational diabetes may alter a woman's risk factor from low to moderate, or from moderate to high.

PRECONCEPTUAL SCREENING, COUNSELING, AND TREATMENT

Genetic Evaluation

If a woman has borne a child with a birth defect, or if she has experienced a miscarriage in which the fetus was abnormal, or if she or her husband has a family history of genetic problems, a prepregnancy chromosome study is advised. This work is supervised by a geneticist, a physician specializing in the study of hereditary traits. To do a chromosome study, or karyotype, cells are obtained from the blood or skin. These cells are then cultured and grown so that they can be examined. The painstaking process takes about five or six weeks to complete. Photographs are taken of the chromosomes and these are cut out in order to match the pairs. In this way, the examiner can determine whether there are missing, extra, or abnormal chromosomes. By performing a karyotype on both parents, the geneticist can advise the couple as to the probability of a hereditary disorder occurring among their offspring. (Virginia Apgar's *Is My Baby All Right?* is an excellent sourcebook on hereditary defects.)

Physical Examination

It is recommended that, after a spontaneous abortion, a woman wait until she has had at least two normal menstrual periods before trying to conceive again. After a stillbirth, she may need more time to recover both physically and emotionally. During that time, the woman should have a complete physical examination to determine if any underlying condition, such as latent diabetes or an incompetent cervix is present. If she has had more than one miscarriage, an endocrine study is advised to discover whether there is a problem with her thyroid, adrenal, or pituitary glands.

Conditions like those mentioned above can frequently be corrected or improved sufficiently to allow a healthy pregnancy. For example, with careful monitoring of diet and medication, a diabetic woman can give birth to a healthy child. Only a few years ago, this was almost impossible. (When thinking of the great strides taken in the past few years, it is quite humbling to realize what is to come. Researchers are currently working with animals in attempts to perform fetal surgery, correcting certain defects before birth.)

As mentioned in Chapter Six, an incompetent cervix can be corrected by means of the Shirodkar procedure. During early pregnancy, a suture is placed around the cervical opening to prevent premature dilatation. The suture is removed at the first sign of labor, so that the birth can proceed normally.

If an endocrine study reveals a lack or excess of a particular hormone, therapy can be instituted before the next pregnancy. If the physical exam indicates that the woman is either underweight or overweight, nutritional counseling is advised.

Women who weigh less than 112 pounds experience premature labor at a rate that is three times that of women who weigh more than 126 pounds.

Besides counseling the woman regarding her weight, her complete nutritional status should be evaluated and recommendations should be made. She also should receive information on the vitamin, mineral, caloric, protein and other nutrient requirements of pregnancy. Studies have shown that placental insufficiency and toxemia are related to poor nutrition. Malnutrition can also cause or increase the severity of birth defects.

Research has shown that LSD and other mind-altering drugs cause chromosomal abnormalities in either the mother or the father. These defective chromosomes can be passed to the unborn child. A high intake of caffeine—over 400 milligrams per day—on the part of either parent before conception increases the risk of first trimester abortion. (Caffeine is found in coffee, tea, chocolates, and most soft drinks. A cup of coffee contains from 120 to 150 milligrams of caffeine. American-brewed tea contains a little less than coffee.)

Preconceptual Counseling

Preconceptual counseling should include the father, emphasizing his role in the health of the child. Studies on the effect of the man's nutritional status are not available, but it would seem likely that a healthy man would produce healthy sperm, and vice-versa.

A preconceptual examination should also reveal whether either parent is exposed to potentially harmful substances, such as cigarette smoke, anesthesia, radiation, or industrial pollution. All of these have been implicated as being detrimental to the unborn child and should be avoided both before and during pregnancy.

Psychosocial Evaluation and Counseling

As explained in Chapter Six, emotional factors seem to be involved for the majority of women who experience habitual abortion. In *Pregnancy: The Psychological Experience*, Arthur and Libby Colman propose that the psychological factors that seem to contribute to habitual miscarriage may be the result of a poor adjustment to the first and subsequent abortions.

In *Modern Perspectives In Psycho-obstetrics*, Edward Mann notes that the habitual aborter tends to be extremely dependent, especially on her mother, and may have lacked an effective father figure. Mann's observations would indicate that any emotional factors involved in miscarriage were present before the first pregnancy. He had an 80 percent success rate in treating habitual aborters through counseling and support. His results make it imperative that a preconceptual evaluation include a determination of the woman's psychosocial background, along with a plan for helping her meet her support needs during pregnancy.

PRENATAL SCREENING AND TREATMENT

Routine Assessment

At the first prenatal checkup blood will be drawn to determine the woman's blood type and Rh factor, as well as to check for anemia, diabetes, and venereal diseases, which can be hazardous to the unborn child. Each time the woman visits her doctor's office or clinic, her blood pressure will be checked to screen for toxemia or gestational hypertension, both of which are complications of pregnancy that threaten the mother and child if not treated. Bedrest remains the most effective treatment at present.

The woman's urine will be tested at each visit to check for the presence of sugar, an indication of diabetes, which can usually be controlled through diet and medication. The urine test will also reveal the presence of albumin if the woman has toxemia. Certain infections can also be detected through urinalysis.

The baby's gestational age is usually determined by combining the date of the last menstrual period, the date movement is first felt, uterine measurement, and a pelvic exam. By listening to the baby's heartbeat, the examiner can determine much about the baby's age and health, and how he is faring in the present uterine environment.

Special Tests

Sonography is becoming more popular as a technique for assessing fetal size, age, and position, as well as determining the size and location of the placenta. This test can also detect some physical abnormalities. Utilizing ultrasound waves that bounce off solid objects, sonography is presently considered noninvasive and safe to both mother and fetus, but there is controversy over this. Ultrasound has almost replaced x-ray in many fields of medicine, including obstetrics. (Although potential hazards, if any, of sonography are unknown, the dangers of x-ray are clear. Even so, in late pregnancy, it may be necessary to use x-ray to make an exact determination of fetal size, age, and position.)

When an ultrasound test is done, the woman's abdomen is coated with an oil or jelly-like substance. An instrument that may look like a wand, a microphone, a gun, or a box, is rubbed along her abdomen, emitting ultrasound waves. The image of the baby can be seen on a video screen. His movements can be seen, and even the beating heart can be detected. (One father swore that the baby waved at him.)

Estriol is a substance produced by the placenta and excreted in the urine. Consistent urine estriol levels are a sign of fetal well-being. In a high-risk pregnancy, serial tests are done to check for a drop in the estriol level, which may indicate fetal problems, and even death.

During pregnancy the urine also contains human chorionic gonadotrophin (HCG). Patients with threatened abortions have low HCG levels, while those with diabetes, toxemia, or Rh isoimmunization have high levels.

Studies of maternal blood enzymes can give significant clues to fetal well-being. Another important test is the measurement of the blood Rh titer, or level of Rh antibodies. If the mother's blood is Rh negative and the father's is Rh positive, there is a risk of Rh isoimmunization leading to erythroblastosis. By monitoring the blood titer, the physician can know if a blood exchange, which can now be done before birth, is necessary.

Amniocentesis involves inserting a needle through the woman's abdominal wall and into the uterus to withdraw amniotic fluid for examination. The fluid can reveal a number of genetic defects, as well as the presence of blood, infection, or meconium, all of which would alert the physician to a probable problem. (Meconium is a dark, tarry substance that accumulates in the fetal colon and is excreted after birth as the first stool. Its release before birth can mean that the baby has been under stress and may not be receiving enough oxygen.) The presence of blood or meconium in the fluid can be detected almost immediately. Infection may take a few days. A chromosomal study will take five or six weeks.

A nonstress test can reveal important information about the baby's intrauterine environment and his ability to withstand labor. The test usually involves attaching electrodes to the woman's abdomen to monitor the rate and quality of the fetal heartbeat. If the nonstress is positive, it indicates possible problems, and a stress, or oxytocin challenge test (OCT), is done.

Carried out in the hospital's labor and delivery unit, an OCT involves giving the woman an intravenous solution of

Pitocin to stimulate uterine contractions. When the contractions are coming every three to five minutes, an electronic monitor is used to check the rate and rhythm and quality of the fetal heartbeat. If the test is negative, the baby should do well for at least another week in the uterus, at which time another OCT is done. A positive stress test indicates the need for prompt delivery either by induction or Cesarean delivery.

Other tests may be done in a high-risk pregnancy, but the above are among the most common.

LABOR AND DELIVERY:
MONITORING AND INTERVENTION

Many of the measures used to monitor and intervene in a high-risk labor are mentioned in Chapters Two, Six, and Seven. These include hospitalization and bedrest for signs of threatened abortion or premature labor, electronic monitoring of the fetal heart and uterine contractions, and watchful waiting. As mentioned earlier, new drugs are being developed and tested for the prevention of premature labor. One of these, Ritrodine, has just gained FDA approval for use in inhibiting labor. Other promising developments that we can expect in the future include a fetoscope to allow the doctor to view the fetus through a small hole in the woman's abdomen, drugs given directly to the fetus to fight infection and other diseases, and fetal surgery for the correction of physical abnormalities. Attempts at fetal surgery have so far been unsuccessful because they always cause labor to begin. Perhaps with drugs like Ritrodine this problem can be overcome. (*Author's Note:* Just before publication of this book, surgery was successfully done to correct a bladder defect in a fetus.)

Sonography or x-ray might be used during labor to determine the advisability of Cesarean delivery. As the cervix begins to dilate, a sample of blood can be obtained from the baby's scalp. This blood is examined to determine the pH, or acid-alkaline balance, which will reveal the level of fetal oxygenation. A progressive drop in pH, determined through several blood samples, is a danger sign, indicating the need for immediate delivery.

During the labor, specific maternal diseases which jeopardize the fetus, such as diabetes, kidney disease, infection, and cardiovascular disease are monitored—as in pregnancy—in accordance with the recommended treatment for each problem. Doctors want to avoid as much as possible any medications or procedures that may harm the baby. The ultimate question in these cases is, "Do the benefits of treatment outweigh the risks?"

From this description of the more common procedures and tests used in high-risk pregnancies, it is clear that these women are not candidates for home delivery, and that the services of a qualified obstetrician should be sought. Besides finding a doctor to meet the physiological needs of pregnancy, these couples should seek early contact with a certified childbirth educator to help meet their educational and support needs throughout the pregnancy.

"Instead of seeing myself sending out birth announcements, I would visualize myself sending letters explaining how and why we had lost another baby. And then I'd think, 'Aggie, you're out of your tree. You didn't lose Keri, and you didn't lose Michael, and you're not going to lose this one." Aggie was talking about her eighth pregnancy, five of which had already ended in stillbirth or miscarriage. Even though she had two healthy children, she just could not let herself believe that she would be lucky, or blessed, again. The pregnancies that follow fetal loss are difficult. If the woman miscarried at three months in the previous pregnancy, she and her spouse will hold their breath until the fourth month of this pregnancy. Then they sigh and say, "We're going to make it." But, if the baby was stillborn, they continue to live in doubt and fear until they hold the squirming, crying, breathing baby in their arms.

During their second pregnancy, Richard said, "All the time my wife had a gnawing fear of losing this precious new life inside her." Cathy's fears were even greater: "I didn't know if I could carry a baby full term, or if it would be normal if I did."

But, as Richard describes it, "The second go-around was a charmed nine months. We both were so proud of our new blue-eyed, red-headed daughter, Heather. Yet, we wondered what that first, fragile life would have been like had it been born. Such thoughts still cross our minds to this day."

The emotional impact of a previous loss on a subsequent pregnancy is best described by the parents. Here Aggie talks about her fourth pregnancy, after having lost three babies to miscarriage and stillbirth:

"We tried many obstetricians, but we always felt manipulated and controlled, just like in the first two pregnancies. Finally, through a childbirth educator, we found a doctor we really liked and respected.

"The pregnancy was beautiful. It was easy. But through the whole thing we never believed we were having a baby. Our Lamaze teacher told us later that we were the only ones in the class who never said, 'After the baby is born . . . ' We always said, 'When we go to the hospital.' We never once mentioned having a baby. We never set up the room. We never got anything done. We just let everything ride.

"During our last Lamaze class I began having contractions. We stopped by the house to pick up some things. When we got to the hospital at eleven o'clock I was two centimeters dilated. Keri was born at one o'clock. The first words out of our mouths were 'Is she alive?'

"The nurse must have thought we were crazy. She said, 'Of course, she's alive.'

"We were so proud of our baby, Keri, and so proud of ourselves—we did it!"

But Aggie and Allen's problems did not end there. Although Keri was, and is, a healthy girl, their next pregnancy ended in a miscarriage due to an IUD. Aggie said, "In the hospital I had that old feeling that I was not in control of myself."

After the miscarriage, extensive surgery was done and Aggie was told she could not have any more children. The doctor strongly urged a hysterectomy after Aggie had time to recuperate. But, in the interim, she became pregnant again.

Throughout this pregnancy, Aggie and Allen maintained an attitude of wait-and-see. They told no one, except a few close friends, until the pregnancy was obvious. Aggie signed a contract to teach school. She felt that the pregnancy would not last. Even when the baby's movement could be felt, she did not let herself believe that this time things would be all right. There were several bad bouts with threatened abortion and premature labor, all of which reinforced her feelings of pessimism. By the time that Aggie and Allen were seven months pregnant, they decided to go on and enroll in my Lamaze classes, just in case. After all, even a premature birth is preceded by labor.

During the classes, they sat quietly, aloof and introverted—the exact opposite of Aggie's nature. This is the way most couples act in prepared childbirth classes if they have experienced a previous infant death. My main concern was that Aggie never talked about the baby and had no plans to take home a living child. Ordinarily parents begin thinking of the baby as a person, and of themselves as that person's parents, in the second trimester. But, Aggie was stuck in the emotional characteristics of the first trimester—the phase of trying to accept the reality of the pregnancy.

When she went into labor, real labor, at last, I drove over to Aggie's house. We sat and drank tea and talked about the baby. She said, "You know, I just realized for the first time that I'll be bringing home a live baby again." And that is exactly what she and Allen did. Michael Allen was welcomed home with the ceremony befitting a miracle baby.

Three years later, Aggie and Allen were surprised to find themselves pregnant again. "We didn't want to go through anymore. We had never had two successful pregnancies in a row. The last one was successful, so this one couldn't be. Again, when I was thinking about writing a birth announcement, I thought about sending that letter of explanation."

This pregnancy was uneventful, except for the fact that it produced the healthy and much loved Kristi. Aggie summed up her feelings about miscarriage and stillbirth as follows: "When you've lost a child it's always there. It's like a scar—you can't get rid of it. It might fade, but it's still there."

Always there, too, are the feelings of failure and inadequacy. Medical explanations for fetal loss include terms like incompetent cervix, inadequate pelvis, defective germ plasm. Those adjectives—incompetent, inadequate, defective— remain to haunt the woman throughout subsequent pregnancies. To her they are more than a diagnosis—they are her.

Many health professionals try to assure the woman by telling her the baby would not have been normal had he survived. Instead of giving her peace, this intensifies her fears, especially during the next pregnancy. How does she know she can carry a baby to term? And if she does, will he be some sort of monster?

These expectant parents need emotional support from the health care team, as well as from friends and family. If un-answered questions remain from the previous pregnancy, they should be encouraged and helped to find clear, concise expla-nations. ·

UNRESOLVED GRIEF

An emotional complication for some pregnant couples is unresolved grief. If a mother or father did not complete the grieving process after losing their baby, and did not reach the stage of acceptance before starting a new pregnancy, there may be serious problems. Emanuel Lewis, consultant psychiatrist of the Department of Child and Family Psychiatry at London's Charing Cross Hospital, writes that failure to mourn after a stillbirth can result in a psychotic breakdown. There can be severe emotional problems for the entire family.

One mother who had lost her first baby at birth had never cried over her loss. She fell victim to the belief that tears are a sign of weakness and inability to cope. During her next pregnancy she never spoke about the coming baby. There were no nursery plans and there was no layette. The only sign of her condition was her growing abdomen. When her baby—a healthy boy—was born, she did not want to see or touch him. After three days, her husband finally convinced her to look at their new son. When she saw him she burst into uncontrollable sobbing. The sight of her beautiful, vigorous baby boy brought back a flood of memories she had repressed for so long. Once the dam had broken the tears kept coming and, with professional counseling and the support and patience of her family, she worked through her grief for her firstborn, reconciling herself to the loss. Slowly, she took on the tasks of mothering her son and developed a deep love for him. She will never forget her first baby, but she has accepted his death and given priority to her living child and her husband.

A family who has experienced fetal death requires follow-up, not only by a medical expert, but also by a professional skilled in the psychosocial aspects of perinatal grief. This person may be a nurse, doctor, childbirth educator, minister, or social worker, and should have special training and experience in this area. If the couple is pregnant again, and one or both of them have not resolved their grief, the counselor can help them do so before the birth. She might begin with an explanation of the stages of grief. It will help if she asks the parents to tell what they remember of the pregnancy and birth and aftermath. Since they probably are still in a sort of denial phase, she must take them slowly, step by step, through each phase of grief, until they have accepted the reality of their loss and have learned to deal with it.

The aid of the woman's obstetrician should be sought and her childbirth educator should be informed of the situation in order to further the couple's support system. The nurses who will assist in labor and delivery and in postpartum should also be apprised of the situation.

To answer the question asked in the title of this chapter—"Can we have a healthy baby?"—I offer the following progress report on some of the couples described in this book:

As reported in this chapter, Aggie and Allen have had three healthy babies out of eight pregnancies. Some of the pregnancies were uneventful until the end, and others gave signs of problems throughout. Some of the uneventful pregnancies yielded healthy babies; some did not. Some of the problem pregnancies yielded healthy babies; some did not. But right now, Aggie, Allen, Keri, Michael, and Kristi are doing fine.

Susan and Britt are currently expecting their first child since losing their daughter Ivy at birth. They enrolled early in my childbirth classes, and all three of us are feeling hopeful.

Linda and Tom had a healthy baby girl, Sally, ten months after the stillbirth of their son. Sally is almost as happy about the whole thing as her parents.

Don and Virginia have been through my classes twice since their miscarriages. Both times they produced robust babies.

Richard and Cathy also have had two healthy babies since their miscarriage.

Dana and Mike already had two children when they suffered a miscarriage. Mike has been transferred to another state, and they have not decided if they want to try again to have another baby.

Judith and Neil had several miscarriages before they were able to have a healthy daughter. Since then it appears that Judith may be infertile. (Remember, Judith had a therapeutic abortion, as well as one after a fetus died. She commented, "I wonder sometimes if maybe you only get so many tries at having a baby, and I used up all of mine." I hope not.)

Donna and Mike have not tried again yet. She went back to school to get a degree in nursing. I saw Donna recently. She said, "Expect me any day to show up in your class. We're going to get pregnant soon."

Patti was the woman who had the ectopic pregnancy. As is the case with many of these women, she has been unable to conceive after many years of trying. Patti found a family anyway—she married a widower with four children.

THE ROLE
OF THE HEALTH
PROFESSIONAL

CHAPTER

9

"What do I say? How do I tell them that I feel frustrated, too? They don't know me. I'm just someone in a white uniform. I don't mean anything to them. I feel like I'm intruding, but I want to be there to help.

"It's so easy to go in and rejoice with them when the baby is healthy, but to go in and grieve with them . . . "

For the maternal health professional, fetal death is the ultimate defeat. Even with a severely ill newborn, at least there is a period, however short, of trying to sustain life. But when the breath of life is not present at birth, all the gleaming, up-to-date equipment and the modern miracle drugs stand waiting and useless.

The professional experiences the same stages of grief as the parents—denial, anger, bargaining, depression, and acceptance—but she usually goes through these phases more rapidly. This difference is probably due to several factors, including the fact that this was not her baby, and that she has a multitude of procedures and tasks to perform for this and other patients.

Heather, the nurse who made the statements at the beginning of this chapter, commented on her own reactions to the frequent stillbirths and miscarriages that occur in the high-risk center where she works:

"I went into obstetrics because I was sick of death and dying, but that was a big mistake. I've seen more death around here than I saw in my entire training.

"When we lose a baby I always think, 'What didn't I do?' It feels like someone punched me in the stomach. I feel angry with the doctors for not doing enough, and disappointed in myself.

"It puts me in a lousy position—I grieve for the patient and the person and me. If I had to sum up my feelings, I would use just one word—despair.

"When you write your book, do me a favor: tell them it hurts us, too."

EFFECTIVE COUNSELING:
THE FOUR C'S

The most frequently asked question is, "What can we do to help?" Heather made a special point of asking for concrete ways to help these parents instead of vague theories and principles. To this end, I have summed up the basic components of effective counseling with the four C's: comfort, caring, communication, and continuity. These are not new concepts, but they are easier to remember and put into practice; they pertain to the nurse, the doctor, the childbirth educator, and any other health professional who deals with grieving parents. Following the summary of the four C's of counseling, I will describe more fully how these apply to each phase of care, from prenatal through postpartum.

Comfort

Before the grieving person can focus on his or her emotional recovery, it is imperative that the health care professional meet all the needs for physical comfort. Although the mother has no living child, she still may have a sore perineum from stitches or hemorrhoids. If she carried her child into the second or third trimester, she is likely to have milk, leading to painful engorgement because she has no infant to suckle. Like any new mother, she may be constipated, or she may have difficulty urinating. All these physical needs must be met as early as possible.

Husbands often comment on how concerned the staff is for the wife's physical needs. Indeed, many doctors and nurses find it difficult to focus on anything else. After all, if you are busy with procedures, no one can expect you to talk, too. Unfortunately, the man—whose physical needs may be limited to fatigue and hunger—cannot benefit as much from this behavior. The alert professional will ask him when he last ate, and offer to order a tray for him so that he can eat with his wife. She will suggest that he go home and sleep while his wife naps, or she may offer to set up a cot for him in the patient's room. Showing concern for his physical needs will set the stage for helping him emotionally.

In Chapter Three, Susan could not move past the denial stage into anger until the fourth day. She had delivered her daughter by Cesarean section and was receiving analgesia, which, although necessary for her comfort, interfered with grief. In her case, there may have been no other acceptable choice. This is true where either unacceptable discomfort or hysteria is involved. Otherwise, sedation should be avoided.

If the woman is experiencing pain, the use of relaxation techniques will help reduce it significantly, and helping herself in this way will raise her self-esteem and confidence. Her husband and family members can help with this, boosting their spirits, as well.

Caring

While seeing to the family's physical comfort, a climate of caring can be set through touch, through expressions of concern, and by just being there. The family appreciates the professional who lets them see her human side. Unlike years past, it is now acceptable, and even therapeutic, for the doctor or nurse to shed tears with the bereaved. It is okay to let the family know that you, too, are hurt by their loss—that, in fact, you feel a loss, as well. At the same time, it is imperative that the professional not let her own display of grief overwhelm the family. If you cannot handle your feelings, remove yourself from the patient's presence for a while, asking another professional to care for her. Later, when you have dealt with your own despair and anger, go back and explain why you left. The health professional can serve as an effective role model for the bereaved family, enhancing their ability to handle their own grief.

Caring can be shown by a hand squeeze or a pat on the shoulder. It is evident in words and gestures. It is best expressed by the simple act of being with the family at frequent intervals. In the beginning, they crave privacy, but are fearful of being alone. They cannot handle long visits, nor can they cope with prolonged periods by themselves. Go to them often throughout the day, asking if they need something or if they want to talk. Stay if they seem to need you. If not, tell them approximately when you will return—and make sure you do.

After the family has gone home, a phone call once or twice a week is welcome. At first, they will not talk much. Silence is awkward, and over the phone it is doubly so. Still, just wait and let them find the words they want. Keep the first calls short. After two or three weeks, if the family has not called you on their own, and if you feel they are handling their grief, wait about a month before you call again. At that time, if you feel they are recovering at a normal rate, let the family know that you are available if they should need you, but that you will wait for them to call. You may never hear from them again, but it is likely they will contact you when they begin to plan the next pregnancy, and will want to keep in touch with you throughout that time.

Communication

Some professionals fall into the trap of talking too much— anything to fill the silence. This also allows them to lead the conversation, making sure that no difficult subjects are broached. Aggie suggested that I devote an entire chapter to things *not* to say to grieving parents. Judith echoed the words of her nursing instructor, "Be a thinking person. Never talk if you think anything you say might hurt someone. Think about it."

Judith knew whereof she spoke. She lost several babies, and her doctor said, "Well, if you hadn't had a bunch of abortions . . . " Her "bunch of abortions" included one done after the fetus was confirmed dead and another done when complications of phlebitis and mumps appeared.

On the other hand, if the professional is so afraid of saying the wrong thing, she can fall into the trap of avoiding the subject altogether. It might help to remember that one poorly handled conversation will not ruin a person for life, but if you feel badly about something you said, do try to understand why. If possible, seek out the person and explain your previous inability to handle the situation.

The rule in counseling is to encourage frank expression of feelings and concerns, and to deal openly with whatever is mentioned. Another rule is *never give advice*. What seems right to the professional may not be the answer for the patient. At any rate, it is the client's right and responsibility to make his or her own decisions.

Phrases that encourage open expression include the following:

"How do you feel?" or "How did that make you feel?"	Instead of telling the individual, "You must feel terrible," or "Don't think about it," these questions say that whatever she feels is okay. They focus on what the person thinks, not what she "should" think.
"You look very sad." or "You seem tired."	These are objective observations. Again, they do not say how someone should feel, nor do they presume to know how she feels. They simply describe what the professional sees. In doing so, the door is opened for the individual to confirm or deny—a good start toward examining how she really feels.
"I think I would feel angry and hurt if this happened to me."	I-messages do not intimidate the listener by telling her what she should or must feel. They simply tell her how the speaker feels. Again, this encourages expression of any negative feelings.
"It's going to hurt for a while, but you'll be a little less sad each day. You'll never forget your baby, but you'll be able to live with her memory."	This affirms the pain she is experiencing. It also gives hope for the future. The mourning family needs to see a light at the end of the tunnel, but they do not want Pollyanna promises.
"I'm praying for you."	Christian, Jew, Moslem, Hindu, and even the atheist will appreciate this genuine expression of concern and caring.

Obviously, these are not the only comments that will help, but they offer a starting point in your conversations with grieving parents. In counseling these people, *avoid* the following:

"Don't think about it."

This inhibits healthy grieving and reinforces denial. If they do not think about their loss, they will not develop tools to cope with it.

"You can always have another baby."

But, they wanted *this* baby!

"You should be thankful you have two healthy children at home."
or
"You should be grateful you still have your health."

These statements only serve to reinforce their guilt feelings. Although the mother with other children moves through her grief more quickly, she also knows the true value of what she has lost. She can remember the births of her children and how they cried and smiled and learned to walk and talk. To her the baby may have been more real than to the first-time mother. As one bereaved parent said, "If I lost my mother, would they say, 'Just be thankful you still have your father'?" As for still having her health, a typical response is, "So what?"

"I know just how you feel."

No, you do not. Even if you have miscarried or delivered a stillborn child, this is *their* experience, and you do not know how they feel. To say you do belittles their own claim to grief.

"It's best this way."

Many medical and nursing books describe miscarriage as a "blessing in disguise." (It is interesting to note that this is the only area in which modern obstetrical textbooks editorialize.) The doctor frequently tells the parents that they

are better off this way. But, heart-
break and loss are never better,
and they are not a blessing.

Continuity

Specialization in health care has many advantages, but a distinct
disadvantage is the fragmenting of care, which is especially
harmful to the grieving family. Many hospitals transfer the
bereaved mother to a general medical-surgical floor, away from
the cries of newborns and the joyful coos of their parents and
grandparents. Although this move is intended to help the
patient and to reduce her pain, it is not always effective, serving
rather to isolate her from the nurses who know what she
has been through and who know how to deal with the physical
discomforts of postpartum. It is imperative that she be placed in
an area where the staff has special training in the emotional
and physical care of the grieving, postpartal woman.

Some hospitals have set aside one or two rooms on the
gynecology floor. The grieving mother has privacy here, and she
is away from the noisy postpartum ward, but she still is cared
for by nurses familiar with her needs. An added advantage
to this system is that it gives the staff a chance to become ac-
quainted with the special needs of these bereaved parents. This
is not possible if the patient is transferred to the first available
bed on any ward. By designating special rooms for the woman
who has had a miscarriage or stillbirth, it is possible to avoid
the awkward slips that occur when a careless nurse asks the
mother if she is breastfeeding, or an enthusiastic candy-striper
offers to take a picture of the new family. Many hospitals
code the chart and room by means of a specially colored
sticker.

Continuity involves the participation of all members of
the health-care team: doctor, nurse, childbirth educator, and
social worker. Each member is responsible for giving the others
any information that will help in fostering healthy griefwork.

Studies show that doctors and nurses tend to do incomplete charting on these patients. The doctors, when asked afterwards, seem to have forgotten those patients who have had a stillbirth. Not surprisingly, though not accusingly, the women usually change doctors for the next pregnancy. They express disappointment in the doctor's lack of open interest and concern; also, they prefer to do everything differently this time, just to be sure. Perhaps the most important thing the health professional can do to improve the emotional care of these parents is to deal honestly with her own feelings of failure and frustration. Some hospitals hold a sharing session after a baby has died. This allows the team members to let out their anger and hurt with each other, which enables them to deal more effectively with the patient and her family.

After discharge, a competent childbirth educator, preferably one who has worked with the family during the pregnancy, can serve as one of the best resources for the bereaved couple. She will keep the doctor informed of the family's progress up until the six-week checkup, at which time he can make his own assessment. Most patients express disappointment that their doctors did not call or ask to see them until six weeks after the birth. If it is feasible, an office visit, or at least a phone call, at two weeks could be therapeutic for both doctor and patient.

Referral to a self-help group is the answer for many grieving parents. Listening Parents, a support group based in Tennessee, trains parents who have lost a baby to counsel newly-bereaved parents. They also have provided health professionals with a complete list of objectives in counseling these couples, as well as a thorough bibliography. Listening Parents can be contacted by writing PEPD (Parents Experiencing Perinatal Death), P.O. Box 38445, Germantown, Tennessee. Please include a self-addressed, stamped envelope—this is a non-profit group.

The Four C's of counseling are applicable to all phases of maternity care. For the parents who lose a baby, the professional care and support begins in early pregnancy and continues until they have adjusted to their loss and resumed their normal activities.

ANTICIPATORY GUIDANCE

Most expectant parents fear that their baby will be born with a physical or mental defect. They may hesitate at first to bring up the subject in the childbirth education classroom for fear of worrying the other parents. But it does, and should come up in class.

In early pregnancy classes, the topic of miscarriage usually arises, but parents rarely mention the possibility of a stillbirth. Occasionally a husband will express concern that his wife may die in childbirth, but somehow it is inconceivable that a fully developed baby could die at or before birth. This means the parents may be totally unprepared to cope with a stillbirth.

The prenatal classroom is probably the best place to provide anticipatory guidance for every expectant couple. The teacher can introduce the topic of "Unexpected Complications," asking the class to describe some of their fears about the birth, while she lists them on the board. They usually will mention pain, prolonged labor, Cesarean birth, and "something wrong with the baby." If they do not cite this possibility, the teacher can do so gently by saying, "Some men worry that their wives will die or be injured in giving birth, and some women fear that the baby will die, or will have a deformity. Have these thoughts crossed your minds?"

The class should then be assured that the risk of stillbirth is only one or two percent, and that it is even lower for prepared couples, but that the purpose of childbirth education is to prepare parents to deal with every possibility.

After compiling the list of fears and concerns, the teacher should divide the class into small groups of four to six people and ask them to list the role of the husband and of the wife in each of the situations. This activity will encourage them to consider the possibility of problems, and will give them a head-start in dealing with any that do arise.

The topic of miscarriage can be dealt with in early prenatal classes. The childbirth educator should teach parents the signs of labor, as well as warning signs, such as bleeding, abdominal pain, and decreased fetal movement. Besides telling them to call the doctor or hospital, she should ask them to get in touch with her if there are problems. Many of these couples miscarry and never show up for the third trimester Lamaze or Bradley classes. The teacher usually assumes they lost interest, when in reality they needed her, but did not know she would be able to help.

Sometimes the subject of stillbirth is introduced in the class through the painful experience of one of the class members. If a couple delivers a stillborn baby before the class series is completed, it is important to be honest with the other members, explaining briefly what happened, and how the parents are doing. The floor should then be opened for comments. After five or ten minutes of expressing how they feel, the class members should be encouraged to think of some ways they can help this couple. Having something positive to do will reduce their fear and helplessness, and such acts of kindness will help boost the self-esteem of the grieving couple.

SUPPORT IN LABOR AND DELIVERY

Even when the evidence is overwhelming, the pregnant woman rarely believes the baby is *really* dead. She alternates between expecting to feel the baby move and realizing that she never will. Some refer to the belief that all babies slow down before labor starts, holding on to this myth as a last hope.

Some women express great fear that a staff member who does not know of her problem may enter the room and try to listen to the baby's heartbeat. The couple does not want to have to explain to each person that their baby is dead. A gentle reference to their situation will reaffirm the reality of the loss, while assuring them that you know what is happening.

To the couple experiencing fetal death, the purpose of the entire pregnancy is wiped out. They face an empty, futile, joyless labor. Since the normal expectations in labor and delivery are of joy, this senseless loss is incongruous to both the parents and the staff.

Some women become model patients, trying not to give any further problems to anyone. Others ask to be asleep, begging the doctor to "take" the baby. Nonproductive pain is less tolerable than pain with a purpose. Since drugs cannot hurt the baby, the woman feels that, if the nurse or doctor really cared, they would give her something. Some will call frequently for help, crying and moaning. Since studies have indicated that frequent requests for medications may be an attempt to get the attention of the staff, it seems reasonable that, by spending more time with the woman, the doctor or nurse can reduce her need for medication, along with her discomfort and fear. A difficult labor with little nursing help will only add insult to injury. These women greatly need the routine physical comfort measures and should never be left alone in active labor.

The father usually feels impotent. Give him specific ways to help his wife. By encouraging him to stay with her and to administer comfort measures, he will feel more important to his wife, and will be able to look back and say, "I did everything I could." Just like his wife, he is suffering a terrible blow to his self-esteem and needs to reassure himself of his own worth. Helping relieve his wife's discomfort and fear will be an important first step toward his own recovery.

Most of these couples want to be together in the delivery room. Few are allowed to do so. Again, it is important that the husband have the choice of supporting his wife during this difficult time, and that she be able to comfort him as well. No one should be coerced to share the birth, but the opportunity should be offered.

The nurse should ask about the father's needs each time she checks on the mother. Recognize that, if he is left in the waiting room, he will meet and talk with other fathers. This is quite difficult. It may help to offer him a separate room where he can rest at intervals during the labor.

The delivery of a dead baby is completely absent of the most prominent features of a normal birth: joy and noise. The limp baby is quickly delivered, the cord is cut, and the child is wrapped and removed from the room. Emanuel Lewis refers to this as the "rugby pass."

The parents strain to hear cries, still not believing the truth, but all they hear are hurried resuscitation attempts, followed by a heavy silence. Often they do not even notice that the baby has been removed from the room. If the mother has been anesthetized for the birth, this reinforces the "nonevent" and the nonexistence of the child.

As previously stated, the staff moves quickly through the stages of grief:

Denial	"Maybe someone else can find the fetal heartbeat."
Anger	"Why doesn't someone fix this machine?!"
Bargaining	"Maybe if we change the mother's position, or re-adjust the monitor."
Depression	"We can't do anymore. It's hopeless."
Acceptance	"Okay, so the baby is dead. But, the parents need our help."

As Aggie described in Chapter Two, families resent the dehumanized, conveyor-belt treatment, procedures, and medications that are given without explanation or consent. This is a complaint of many women who have had healthy babies, but the pain and humiliation is magnified when the baby is dead.

In *Birth*, Caterine Milinaire includes the story of Joan Weiner, whose daughter was born at the home of her doctor:

"She didn't cry, except for a gurgle that was fluid being sucked out of her lungs by the straining of the doctor. After that, total stillness. No life. No cry of shock or pain as adrenaline was shot directly into her heart, piercing the bluish doll's chest. There was nobody home. The driver had gone, leaving us to cry over the perfect, unblemished, never-to-be-used vehicle.

"Anyway, it was easier to have this thing go down in a home, rather than in a hospital. I was surrounded by the people who loved me, who cried with me and who didn't make me feel ashamed over so much emotion. I wasn't shut away in a sterile, little room . . . "

POSTPARTAL SUPPORT

If the baby died before the onset of labor, the parents may already have begun to deal with their grief. For this reason, it may surprise the health professional to hear a mother or father ask the doctor to spank the baby to see if it will cry. Even though they previously had moved from shock and denial into other stages of grief, it is natural that the age-old moment of birth might bring on some illogical hopes.

Having faced their loss ahead of time, the couple probably will move more quickly through the first stages of grief after the birth. Many of the suggestions already given in this chapter and throughout the book pertain to the role of the health professional during postpartum. The following are further suggestions for helping the family cope after the miscarriage or stillbirth:

• Identify the patient as a bereaved mother, whether through a coding system or the use of a special room. This should be done inconspicuously, so that she does not feel branded or labeled. In a high-risk maternity center, it is feasible to set aside a special room. Smaller hospitals might use a coding system, such as a purple tag on the Kardex, chart, and room door.

• Assign the same nurses to the patient's care throughout

her hospital stay. One person should take the responsibility for following up the recovery after she is released from the hospital. This same nurse should organize a return discussion with the staff several weeks after the birth. At this time they can clear up any unanswered questions or misconceptions.

• Arrange for a private room. This will make it easier to cry and will facilitate flexible visiting hours.

• Sleep is rare and precious. Do not awaken the woman for routine procedures.

• Decisions may be difficult for her to make. Prompt her by offering food, drink, and so on. Avoid fostering overdependence, but recognize the normal characteristics and needs of the "taking in" phase that precede "taking hold." All new mothers need to be mothered. The feelings of unworthiness that the bereaved woman has can be eased by having others do things for her, making her feel that she is indeed worthy of love and concern.

• Because decisions are difficult and she is vulnerable, the mother may consent readily to a proposed tubal ligation. This can be a means of punishing herself for perceived guilt. It is imperative that any decisions regarding permanent sterilization be postponed until her physical and emotional recovery is complete.

• Recognize any anger toward you as healthy expressions of grief, not personal attacks.

• Ask about the labor. All new parents have a tremendous need to describe over and over what happened. In this case, the retelling validates the entire pregnancy and birth. In the case of prepared couples, it affirms the mother's womanliness and the father's strength.

• Help the parents obtain clear information regarding what happened. Explanations should be simple and concise. They probably will need to be repeated more than once. Offer to help obtain genetic counseling if indicated.

• Offer the parents a chance to see the baby. Let *them*

decide. Each parent should make this decision individually. The staff often fears that the parents will overreact to the sight of their dead baby, but this may be a form of self-protection on the part of the professionals. Even if the baby is deformed, it will not be as bad as what the parents will conjure up in their minds in years to come if they do not see their child. If a strong reaction does occur, it indicates a great need for letting out pent-up emotions. Marshall Klaus and John Kennel comment that touching and seeing facilitates healthy grieving. Through physical bonding with the dead baby, they can let go of their fantasy child.

• Before letting the parents see the child, explain that, due to circulatory differences, the baby is not pale, but red. The skin may be peeling, and the head might be more molded than they expected. If an abnormality exists, prepare them for this, as well. When they see the child, point out unique and/or familial features. Use the baby's name, and say "he" or "she" instead of "it." Offer them time alone with their child. Respect the specialness of this child to his parents.

• Assist the couple with any forms. Usually there is an autopsy consent. The stillbirth certificate is sent to the state capital and a copy can be obtained from the Bureau of Vital Statistics. Although it is not required to name the child, it will help facilitate grieving if they do.

• See to it that the family's cultural and spiritual needs are met and respected. Offer to contact their minister, priest, or rabbi. A medicated parent, or one who is in shock, may forget to ask that the baby be baptized, so the professional should inquire about this.

• Ask the couple about their preference for burial, explaining the options. Many are unaware that they can arrange a private funeral. Others have ghastly thoughts about what a hospital burial entails. Explain these alternatives as they exist in your area. (A maternity nurse pointed out that, although many authors feel it is best for the couple to arrange a funeral service, some parents are relieved when they find out that the hospital will take care of this for them. Some cannot afford a private burial; others cannot face one.)

● If the parents had brought baby clothers with them to the hospital, ask if they would like to have the baby dressed in them, or do it themselves, for the burial.

● Recognize pathological grief, and refer the person to the appropriate mental health professional. Warning signs include severe psychosomatic reactions, delayed emotional response, exaggerated behavioral changes, detrimental behavior, or prolonged or intense grief.

Before closing this chapter, it is important to note that bereaved parents expressed gratitude for the thoughtfulness of nurses in many cases. Health professionals always have the interests of the patient at heart, but sometimes they are unsure as to how to fulfill those needs. That is what this chapter has tried to do—offer a guide for helping the grieving couple return to a normal, healthy state.

Ending the conspiracy of silence should begin with those best equipped to do so—the health professionals. By recognizing birth and death as integral parts of the natural life cycle of the family, we can take the first, and most important, step toward healing the wounds of grief.

GLOSSARY

Abortion. Birth of a nonviable fetus.

Abruptio placenta. Premature separation of the placenta from the uterine wall.

Amniotic sac. Also called bag of waters. Membranous sac containing amniotic fluid which surrounds and protects the unborn baby.

Anesthesia. Drug given to cause loss of sensation.

Anoxia. Lack of oxygen in the body. Often used interchangeably with the term *hypoxia.*

Cervix. Lower, narrow portion of uterus. Opens during labor to allow passage of baby into vagina.

Cesarean. Delivery of baby through an incision in the abdominal wall of the mother.

Conceptus. Fetus.

Congenital. Pertaining to a condition present at birth.

Contraction. The tightening and shortening of a muscle, followed by relaxation. Uterine contractions work to dilate the cervix and push out the baby.

Crowning. Appearance of baby's head at the vaginal opening.

D and C. Dilatation and curettage. The manual opening of the cervix in order to curette, or scrape out, the uterus.

Dilatation. The opening of the cervix. Measured in centimeters, with ten centimeters being complete.

Ectopic pregnancy. Pregnancy outside of the uterus. Occurs when implantation takes place in another location, such as the Fallopian tube.

Effacement. Shortening and thinning of cervix in order to transfer the thickness of muscle to the upper portion of the uterus during labor. Measured in percentage, with 100 percent being complete.

Embryo. Name for the unborn child during first two months.

Erythroblastosis. An isoimmune disease in which the fetal blood is destroyed by antibodies in the maternal blood. Occurs only in women who are Rh negative and whose babies are Rh positive.

Fallopian tubes. Hollow tubes on either side of uterus. Carry egg from ovary to uterus. Common site of ectopic pregnancy.

Fertilization. Conception. The union of the sperm and the egg to form an embryo.

Fetus. Name for unborn child during last seven months of pregnancy.

Genetic. Refers to conditions that are hereditary.

Gestation. Refers to the period of time when the fetus is developing in the uterus.

Hemorrhage. Severe, uncontrolled bleeding.

Hyaline membrane disease. Commonly known as Respiratory Distress Syndrome (RDS), this condition afflicts many premature babies, whose lungs are not yet capable of sustaining respiration.

Hypoxia. A deficiency of oxygen in the body. (See *Anoxia.*)

Implantation. Attachment of fertilized egg to lining of uterus. Occurs on about the sixth day.

Incomplete abortion. Abortion in which a portion of the products of conception, that is, the fetus, amniotic sac, or placenta, are retained.

Induced abortion. Abortion that is intentionally accomplished through mechanical or medical means.

Inevitable abortion. Abortion which is in the process of happening, and cannot be stopped.

Infiltrate. Occurs when an IV is not properly in place and the fluid seeps into the surrounding tissues.

IV. Intravenous. Refers to medication or other fluids administered through a vein.

Membranes. Amniotic sac.

Miscarriage. Lay term which usually refers to the birth of a nonviable baby after three months and before seven months gestation. Used interchangeably with "abortion."

Missed abortion. Occurs when the fetus dies, but is not expelled by the woman's body. May not be detected for several weeks.

Neonatal. Having to do with the neonate, or newborn.

Nonviable. Not capable of sustaining life. Although 28 weeks gestation is considered to be the point of viability, many babies born much earlier have survived.

Ovum. Egg. The female's contribution to conception.

Pitocin. A synthetic hormone that mimics oxytocin, stimulating the uterus to contract. Sometimes used to induce or augment labor, as well as to prevent postpartum hemorrhage.

Placenta. Afterbirth. The liver-like organ that provides for the transfer of oxygen and nutrients from mother to child and waste products from child to mother. It is expelled after the birth.

Placenta previa. Implantation of placenta near or over the cervix.

Postpartum. The six-week period following the birth.

Premature birth. Birth of a live infant at less than thirty-seven weeks gestation. Sometimes applied to any infant weighing less than 5 lb. 8 oz. at birth. Prematurity is the major cause of neonatal death.

Presenting part. The part of the baby that is closest to the cervix and will be born first.

Prolapsed cord. Refers to a situation in which the umbilical cord drops in front of the presenting part, causing danger of compression of the cord and cutting off the baby's supply of blood and oxygen.

Sperm. The male reproductive cell.

Spontaneous abortion. Expulsion of a nonviable fetus due to natural causes.

Station. The level of the presenting part in relation to the mother's pelvic bones, usually measured in centimeters.

Stillbirth. Birth in which the baby is not alive.

Threatened abortion. Situation in which woman has signs of miscarriage, such as cramping and vaginal bleeding, but little or no cervical dilatation has occurred, and no tissue has been passed.

Therapeutic abortion. Abortion induced to prevent serious damage to the mother's health. May also refer to an abortion done due to the diagnosis of a defect in the unborn child.

Toxemia. Also called preeclampsia. Condition characterized by onset of high blood pressure, excess swelling, and the presence of albumin in the urine. Occurs only after the twentieth week of pregnancy. Usual treatment is bedrest. Untreated, it may lead to eclampsia, which is characterized by convulsions.

Trimester. Period of three months.

Ultrasound. Diagnostic test using ultrasound waves to visualize the fetus and placenta.

Umbilical cord. About twenty-one inches long, this coiled cord provides the transport of oxygen and nutrients from the placenta to the child and waste products from the child to the placenta.

Uterus. Womb. Hollow, muscular organ that receives, protects, and nourishes the fetus for nine months, at which time it contracts to open the cervix and push the child out through the vagina.

Vagina. Birth canal. Opening in the female body that allows the male to insert his penis and deposit sperm. Opening through which child is born. About five inches long, its inner walls are built like an accordion, able to expand or contract to accommodate the size of whatever it holds.

Viable. Capable of sustaining life.

BIBLIOGRAPHY

The following list includes references used in writing this book, as well as recommended reading. Parents who read this list may not want to look up the technical books and journal articles, but will find the sources marked with an asterisk (*) very helpful and interesting.

*Apgar, Virginia, *Is My Baby All Right?* New York: Simon and Schuster, 1974.

*Brewer, Gail, *What Every Pregnant Woman Should Know.* New York: Random House, 1972.

*Borg, Susan and Judith Lasker. *When Pregnancy Fails.* Beacon, 1980.

Butler, "Cigarette Smoking," *Perinatal Press,* May-June 1976. Originally published in *OB/GYN Observer,* no. 5 (1976).

Caldeyro-Barcia, Roberto, "Some Consequences of Obstetrical Interference," *Birth and the Family Journal,* no. 2 (1975), pp. 34-38.

*Colman, Arthur, and Libby Colman, *Pregnancy: The Psychological Experience.* New York: Bantam, 1977.

Cooper, Joan, "Reactions to Stillbirth: 'End This Conspiracy of Silence,' " *Nursing Mirror,* no. 23, (April, 1980), pp. 31-33.

Davidson, Glen, *Understanding the Death of a Wished-for Child.* Springfield, MA: OGR Service Corp., 1979.

*Elkins, Valmai, *Rights of the Pregnant Parent.* New York: Two Continents Publishing Group, 1976.

Furman, Erna, "The Death of a Newborn: Care of the Parents," *Birth and the Family Journal,* no. 4 (1978), pp. 214-218.

Greenhill, J.P. and Emanuel Freidman, *Biological Principles and Modern Practice of Obstetrics.* Philadelphia: Saunders, 1974.

*Guttmacher, Alan, *Pregnancy, Birth, and Family Planning.* New York: Viking, 1973.

Hallet, Elizabeth, "Birth and Grief," *Birth and the Family Journal,* no. 4 (1974), pp. 18-22.

Kitzinger, Sheila, *Education and Counselling for Childbirth.* London: Balliere Tindall, 1977.

*Kitzinger, Sheila, *Women as Mothers.* London: Fontana, 1978.

Klaus, Marshall, and John Kennel, *Maternal-Infant Bonding.* Saint Louis: C. V. Mosby, 1976.

Kowalski, Karren, and Mary Osborn, "Helping Mothers of Stillborn Infants to Grieve," *The American Journal of Maternal Child Nursing,* no. 1 (1977), pp. 29-32.

Lewis, Emanuel, "The Management of Stillbirth: Coping with an Unreality," *The Lancet,* no. 7986 (1976), pp. 619-620.

Lewis, Emanuel, "Mourning by the Family after a Stillbirth or Neonatal Death," *Archives of Disease in Childhood,* no. 54 (1979), pp. 303-306.

Mann, Edward, "Spontaneous Abortions and Miscarriage," *Modern Perspectives in Psycho-Obstetrics.* Edited by John Howells. New York: Brunner/Mazell Publishers, 1972.

Manning, F. A. and C. Feyerabend, "Smoking and the Fetus," *Briefs,* January 1977, pp. 6-7. Originally published as

"Cigarette Smoking and Fetal Breathing Movements," *Obstetrical and Gynecological Survey,* no. 10 (1976), pp. 716.

McLenahan, Irene, "No Baby To Take Home," *American Journal of Nursing,* no. 4 (1962) pp. 70-71.

*Milinaire, Caterine, *Birth,* New York: Harmony Books, 1974.

Parer, J. and Helen Dulocle, eds., "Intrapartum Evaluation of the Fetus," Supplement to the *Journal of Obstetric, Gynecologic, and Neonatal Nursing,* no. 5 (1976).

Pumphrey, John, et al., "Recognizing Your Patients' Spiritual Needs," *Nursing 77,* no. 12 (1977), pp 64-70.

Rinear, Eileen, "Helping the Survivors of Expected Death," *Nursing 75,* no. 3 (1975), pp. 60-65.

Saylor, Dennis, "Nursing Response to Mothers of Stillborn Neonates," *Journal of Obstetric, Gynecologic, and Neonatal Nursing,* no. 4 (1977), pp 39-42.

Schneider, Kathy, and Janet Daniel, "Dealing with Perinatal Death," *Perinatal Press,* no. 7 (1979), pp. 101-105.

Seitz, Pauline, and Louise Warrick, "Perinatal Death: The Grieving Mother," *American Journal of Nursing,* no. 11 (1974), pp. 2028-2033.

Shearer, Madelaine, "Some Deterrents to Objective Evaluation of Fetal Monitors," *Birth and the Family Journal,* no. 2 (1975), pp. 58-62.

Weathersbee, Paul, Larry Olson, and J. Robert Lodge, "Caffeine and Pregnancy: A Retrospective Survey," *Postgraduate Medicine,* no. 3 (1977), pp. 64-69.